# The River Within

CHRISTOPHER BRYANT SSJE

# The River Within

*The Search for God in Depth*

DARTON, LONGMAN AND TODD

First published in 1978
by Darton, Longman and Todd Ltd
89 Lillie Road, London SW6 1UD
© 1978 Christopher Bryant SSJE

ISBN 0 232 51374 0

Printed and bound in Great Britain by
Anchor Brendon Ltd, Tiptree, Essex

Fifth impression 1987

# Contents

# Preface

This book is written in the hope of making a contribution to the working out of a spirituality for the late twentieth century. This aim has inevitably drawn me into the field of psychology. Spiritual writers of the past made use of the psychology current in their own day. The writings of St Augustine, St Bernard and St Teresa of Avila are all deeply psychological. But the old psychologies, despite the profound human insight of some of those who accepted their analysis of human nature, seem unreal today. To talk of human personality and experience in a manner that makes sense to the typical man or woman of the twentieth century it is necessary to go to school with Freud, Jung and many others, to learn their language and to ponder their insights into the dynamics of personality. The response to my *Depth Psychology and Religious Belief* and to lectures, papers and articles given or written during the past ten years has made me realise that many people today, by no means only professing christians, are deeply interested in an exposition of the christian life illuminated by psychology.

My debt to other writers in this field is immensely greater than the comparatively few quotations might appear to indicate. It would be impossible to enumerate the books and authors that have influenced and informed me. A few debts are acknowledged in the text or foot notes, many have no doubt been forgotten. I mention here only two, neither of them unfortunately alive, to whom I am especially indebted: Victor White, particularly his books, *God and the Unconscious* and *Soul and Psyche*, for his use of Jung's ideas to light up the unmapped land between theology and psychology, and Austin Farrer for the depth and clarity of his theological writings.

I am grateful to Darton, Longman and Todd for undertaking to publish the book and in particular to Robin Baird-Smith for his courteously given help, advice and criticism. I am also indebted to Mrs Wendy Robinson for her persistence in urging me to write the book and for valuable criticisms of the first draft. I am grateful also to several members of my community, particularly to Father Martin Smith, for reading and commenting on the first draft.

OXFORD, MAY 1977   CHRISTOPHER BRYANT SSJE

# 1. Introduction

We shall not cease from exploration
And the end of all our exploring
Will be to arrive where we started
And know the place for the first time.

T.S. Eliot, *Little Gidding* ll. 239–242

In his *Myths, Dreams and Mysteries* Mircea Eliade tells the story of an obscure Jewish rabbi, Isaac son of Jekel, who several hundred years ago lived in great poverty in a single-roomed house in Cracow. One night he dreamt vividly of a treasure buried beneath the bridge leading to the royal palace at Prague. Three nights running he dreamt the same dream and, unable to dismiss it from his mind, he determined to make the long journey to Prague on foot in search of the treasure. But when he reached the city he was bitterly disappointed to find the bridge guarded by soldiers and the treasure, if indeed there was a treasure, totally inaccessible. As the rabbi stood there in dejection the captain of the guard took pity on him and asked him what his trouble was. So he related his dream. The captain of the guard laughed. 'You should not pay attention to dreams. Why, only the other night I had a dream about treasure. It was buried in the house of a man I had never heard of, a rabbi named Isaac son of Jekel who lived in Cracow. But no sensible man pays attention to dreams.' The rabbi listened with inward astonishment, he bowed low and thanked the captain. Then he set off with all haste back to Cracow and when he reached home

1

he at once began to dig in the corner of his room behind the stove. Eventually he unearthed a treasure sufficient to end his poverty.

## THE TRIPLE DIALOGUE

The story is a parable told to describe the rabbi's long search for a wisdom that would give meaning to life. The treasure he at last discovered was that of his ancestral faith. He had grown up with it, it was near him all the time, but he did not at all recognise its value. To discover this he had to make a long journey and be directed to it by a stranger who himself did not understand its worth. No doubt the search was more arduous and more complex than the story taken literally implies. Only after days and hours of study and of argument and discussion with the guardians of the christian faith and of assimilation of many ideas from that alien source did he come to perceive the treasure buried deep in his own tradition. Many a modern man and woman brought up in the christian tradition has had to make a similar arduous journey in order in the end to come back with an immensely enriched understanding to the tradition in which he grew up. Some have reached journey's end only after a sojourn, metaphorical or actual, in the east. But I believe even more important than the study of the wisdom of the east is dialogue with the secular thinkers of the west. In fact what I believe is needed is a threefold dialogue: with the gospel which proclaims God's self-disclosure in Jesus Christ, with the spiritual tradition built up by Christians as they wrestled generation after generation with the task of understanding and living out the gospel in a changing world, and with the best minds of today. And in the contemporary dialogue we particularly need to confront the new ideas about man associated with the names of Charles Darwin, Karl Marx and Sigmund Freud. Through these men and their collaborators and successors the consciousness of the educated man of today has been extended by his realisation of his animal ancestry, his social conditioning and his irrational depths. In consequence he tends to find the older writings about man, with only a few

exceptions chiefly among the poets and dramatists, unconvinc-
ing and irrelevant. I believe this triangular dialogue will do a
double service for the twentieth century Christian. First it will
help him to separate the gold from the dross in the inherited
tradition. For the trouble with tradition is its vast amount and
unequal quality. The contemporary dialogue will enable him to
discriminate, it will tell him where in the great house of tradition to dig. Second it will help the teachers and preachers of today to translate the old gospel into an idiom intelligible and
meaningful to people of the twentieth century. This book is
mainly concerned with a tiny part of this dialogue, the dialogue
with psychology and, in particular with depth psychology of
which Freud was the pioneer.

The dialogue with psychology has long been important to
me. Through it I have gained a deeper understanding of the
truth and power of the gospel. At the age of seventeen when feeling my way out of teenage agnosticism I came across William
James' *Varieties of Religious Experience*. The book made me realise
for the first time that religion could be a transforming experience. Some fifteen years later the reading of Jung's *Modern
Man in Search of a Soul*,[1] followed by the reading of several
other of his works, helped me to realise the meaning and relevance of christian doctrines to which I had already given intellectual assent. Some years later I had the good fortune to be
invited to join a small group consisting of clergy and psychoanalysts, which met some four or five times a year to discuss
matters of common concern. Seven years of membership in
this group taught me what I doubt if I could have learnt in any
other way, certainly not from books. Perhaps I could sum up
what I gained from the group as a certain confidence in using
psychology to illuminate christian ideas and experience.
Besides my interest in psychology I have for forty years been
deeply concerned about the christian gospel and the christian
tradition of prayer and the spiritual life. During these years the
three interests have interacted in my mind to the enrichment of
each of them. This book is the fruit of this inner dialogue.

# THE GOSPEL AND THE CHRISTIAN SPIRITUAL TRADITION

The heart of christianity is a gospel, good news. It burst upon the world in first century Palestine as a message about God and his purpose for man. It was a message of hope about a new life available for all who would receive it. It spoke to men's hearts and changed their lives. It was couched inevitably in the language and the ideas current in the Palestine of that day. The good news spoke powerfully to the condition of those who first heard it because it was woven into the background of ideas which they took for granted. The strangeness and the challenge could not be ignored because it met them clothed in assumptions that were familiar and unquestioned. Many of those assumptions, for example about cosmology, about the all-pervasive influence of demons, about the shortly to be expected end of the world, seem to us either mistaken or irrelevant. And so the shared background of ideas which made it easy for the first disciples to understand and respond to the gospel is an obstacle now. If the gospel is to make on people of the twentieth century anything like the impact it made on the men of the first it will have to be interwoven with the beliefs and ideas that are important today. The gospel startled and shocked many good men when it was first proclaimed. It threatened to overthrow long cherished ideas and customs. No faithful translation of the gospel into contemporary idiom could or should defuse its explosive force. The exaltation of poverty in the beatitudes, for example, is likely to scandalise the modern economist who desires to increase his country's gross national product as much as it did the traditional minded Jew who believed that worldly prosperity was a mark of God's blessing. But the cutting edge as well as the liberating power of the gospel can only be preserved if it comes to grips with the discoveries of modern science and the new knowledge which has transformed the outlook of men and women today. If the gospel is true it can have no quarrel with the new knowledge. For myself I believe that preachers of the gospel will find that it gains in clarity and power if they are prepared to listen to modern scientific thought, not uncritically but with a readiness to learn. The preacher and the pastor has much to learn from the behavioural sciences. In particular I think that an important part of the task of restating the gospel must be carried out by a psychology that can explore and interpret experience. For Christianity was an experience before it was a theology. The New Testament is the record of an experience of God mediated through the life, teaching, death and resurrection of Jesus, the Messiah. It was an experience of deliverance from hostile spiritual powers and of a new openness to God and to other men. It was both a deeply personal experience and an experience of warm fellowship with other believers. When St Paul spoke of his fellow believers as those who were in the Messiah or who lived in the Spirit, he was appealing to an experience which both he and his hearers knew, though naturally not all with equal intensity.

Very soon the powerful stream of the original Christian experience which expressed itself in deep devotion to the Lord, in brotherly love, unselfish conduct and courageous witness, flowed into the world of greek thought, fertilising it and in return deriving from it a new intellectual character. The first Christian theologians, St Paul pre-eminent among them, laboured to express their new experience of God in terms of the jewish ideas with which they were familiar. Their successors struggled with the help of the terminology and logical method of greek philosophy to explain the gospel to the greco-roman intellectual world. The faith came to be expressed less in symbol and metaphor and more in doctrinal statements and creeds. This development, inevitable and right, brought solid gains to the Church as Christianity became increasingly integrated with the ideas current in the ancient roman world. But the development brought loss as well as gain. For the more theology becomes intertwined with the thought of one age the less intelligible and the less relevant it will appear to an age whose fundamental assumptions are different. There are many signs today that people in the west are hungry for some experience of God that will give meaning to life; but for the most part they do not expect to find the spiritual food they need in the Church or its gospel. Both are felt to belong to an age that is past and to be out of touch with the contemporary world. Christian faith is supposed to be no more than assent to doctrines formulated long ago and impossible to prove. But if the gospel could be proclaimed and the christian spiritual tradition expressed in an up-to-date idiom without leaving out anything essential I believe these would answer the needs of the twentieth century as effectively as the gospel in its Jewish dress met the needs of the first.

From the first the gospel summoned men to live in two worlds. It promised a new life of intimate fellowship with God to all those who were prepared to pay the price of committing themselves to his kingly rule. But this new life had to be lived in a world where a man must earn a living, discharge the duties of a neighbour and citizen and perhaps those of a husband and father. A spiritual tradition grew up to guide him in the prayer and discipline which were essential if he were to maintain his commitment to God under the pressures of this world. So from the beginning the gospel was embodied in a way of life which was both new and old. It was old because it took over from devout Judaism a tradition of prayer, fasting and almsgiving, of synagogue worship and of reverence for the Old Testament Scriptures. It was new because the good news of God's love and mercy disclosed in the crucified and risen Messiah acted like a powerful, transforming leaven upon the received tradition. The institution of the Eucharist, the commemorative celebration both of the Messiah's last supper with his disciples and of his death and resurrection, early became the focal point of each week. The gospel lit up the Old Testament and enabled christian apostles, evangelists and teachers to discern the things in it which pointed to the Messiah and to choose what to retain of jewish custom and what to drop. The letters of St Paul make it possible for us to trace the beginnings of a distinctively Christian way of life. Later an authoritative selection from the earliest christian writings was brought together and embodied in a book which came to be called the New Testament. A succession of influential books, among them the *Confessions* of St Augustine, the *Imitation of Christ*, the *Pilgrim's Progress*, to name three of the best known, has helped to shape the development of a christian spiritual tradition and enables us to chart its course. Christian spirituality interacting as it must with the surrounding secular culture has always been changing. One of the formative influences upon it has been monasticism whose roots are in judaism but which received a powerful impulse from the paganism and moral laxity of the Roman empire to which it reacted strongly. Certain themes occur and recur in its history. The christian life is seen as a following of Christ, as a journey through life in stages which are marked by growth in union with God's will (the purgative, illuminative and unitive ways), it is seen as a life of prayer and self-renunciation. In the course of centuries a large body of moral, ascetic and mystical theology has been built up as a guide to the learned and devout, as well as many popular methods of devotion and much folk lore which has fed the piety of the unlettered. There is much treasure buried in this vast field but there is much also that is out of date and much that seems misguided.

Before going on to indicate how psychology can shed light on the mass of tradition some brief treatment is demanded of the doctrine of divine providence. This teaching inherited from Judaism and fundamental both to the gospel and to the christian spiritual tradition is a difficulty to many otherwise sympathetic moderns. The doctrine of the active presence of the transcendent God in all that is and all that happens is implied in the teaching of Jesus that the hairs of man's head are numbered, that not a sparrow falls to the ground without the Father's knowledge and care. His injunction to his disciples not to worry about food and drink and dress but to seek the reign of God and trust God to take care of the rest implies God's active providence over human life. The eighteenth century spiritual writer de Caussade[2] may serve to illustrate how this belief in God's providence can be made the keystone of a way of life. He teaches us to see everything that happens as coming to us from the hand of God. God addresses us through the people we meet and the work we do, through our hopes and fears, through our moods and dreams through the good he sends and the evil he permits. De Caussade speaks of the sacrament of the passing moment because in each fleeting moment we are confronted with an opportunity of responding to God who is present in that moment. No experience is so painful, no temptation so strong as to fall outside God's fatherly care.

Many people today, especially those who have been trained in one of the sciences, find this idea of God's active presence throughout the universe unreal, and for two main reasons. The first and principal reason is that modern western civilization tends to ignore the reality of God and we cannot but be influenced by the climate of opinion which surrounds us. The way of life of most moderns tends to leave God out of the reckoning. Churchgoing is looked upon as the hobby of a minority; and even among churchgoers there is small sense that what they are engaged in is closely related to the whole of life. The second reason is the enormous advances that the sciences have made by concentrating on the measurable and ignoring what cannot be measured. The prestige of the scientific method of exact observation and measurement, the framing of a hypothesis to account for the observed phenomena, and the devising of an experiment to verify or falsify the hypothesis is so great as to create the impression that what cannot be scientifically proved – for example the insights of the artist, the musician or the poet – is a doubtful, second class kind of knowledge. The scientist, like the astronomer Laplace, is able to explain area after area of the universe without recourse to God. This is not the place to attempt to prove the reality of God and of his universal providence. There is no proof that can give the kind of certainty that is based on oft-repeated scientific experiment. Perhaps we must say that the evidence pointing to God – for example, the non-self-explanatory existence of the universe or the well-nigh universal belief in God or some transcendent power – is only convincing to those who already have a predisposition to believe. Or perhaps we must say with Buber: 'There are no proofs, only witnesses.' But it is in place to point out that few theologians today would expect the scientist to find particular traces of the action of God in the course of his scientific observations or experiments, any more than they expected the russian astronaut to discover God in the stratosphere.

The scientist remembering Galileo may be a little suspicious that the theologian if he had the power might dictate to the scientist in the scientist's own special domain. But in fact I doubt if any competent theologian could be found who would desire any such thing. Let the late Austin Farrer, a fairly traditional theologian, stand as an example of the way a theologian understands the action of divine providence. Farrer conceives God's creatorhood and providence as supporting and in no way interfering with the creature's proper independence and that of the network of causes and inter-relationships which the scientist labours to understand. 'God not only makes the world', he writes, 'he makes it make itself; or rather, he causes its innumerable constituents to make it. And this in spite of the fact that the constituents are not for the most part intelligent.'[3] He in no way conceives of God as arbitrarily interfering with the proper working of nature's laws. 'The world is so made as to run itself, but every creature it contains is confronted by the omnipotence that made it; is confronted, that is to say, by an inexhaustible power for good and an inexhaustible fund of invention or contrivance'.[4] It is easy, by carefully selecting your evidence, to trace a clear pattern of order running through the universe. But how then are you to account for the disorder, the excessive pain, the evil that is to be found in it? Farrer is very conscious of this problem. He compares God's providence over the universe to the government of a democratic state. 'In the political sphere a hundred per cent success for public order or economic planning is unthinkable so long as individual freedom is given its rights'.[5] There is a kind of democratic principle, a kind of indeterminacy at work in the structure of things. 'In the natural order a hundred per cent success for animal bodies is unthinkable, if the cellular, chemical and atomic systems of which they are composed are to retain their rights and go on being themselves in their own way at every level'.[6] The rights that divine providence designs his creatures to retain correspond with that secular independence which the scientist is concerned to defend against theological interference. But what this book is especially concerned with is the active presence of God within and around each personality. The 'inexhaustible power for good and the inexhaustible fund of invention and contrivance' is present in such a way as to support and not undermine his own proper individuality. God's action may be conceived as a kind of invisible pressure setting a bias towards the choices and decisions which will lead a person to greater freedom and fulfilment. But to see how this might work out it is necessary to listen to the voice of psychology.

## THE DIALOGUE WITH PSYCHOLOGY

There are many psychologies as there are many facets of human nature and many ways of approaching the study of man. Experimental psychology studies man from the outside. It seeks to measure all that is measurable in man. It studies human behaviour and tries to formulate laws governing it. It relies much on statistics and has acquired much new knowledge especially in the sphere of perception, memory and learning. The behaviour of dogs, rats and monkeys has been studied by means of carefully controlled experiments in order to discover laws which might govern human behaviour. Dynamic psychology with which this book will be chiefly concerned studies man's subjectivity. It seeks to understand inner experience and motive. The depth psychologist bases his theories not on measurable behaviour but on the reports people make of their thoughts, feelings, wishes and dreams, checked and authenticated by his own self-scrutiny. The theories and hypotheses of dynamic psychology are extremely difficult to substantiate because of the virtual impossibility of framing an experiment that would not fatally interfere with the facts they were designed to explain. The theories are however framed to account for observed phenomena and are retained, though they may be incapable of scientific proof because they are believed to explain some areas of mental life better than any other. Many christians are uneasy about the tendency of dynamic psychology, partly because its great pioneer, Sigmund Freud, was an atheist and wrote a book about religion called *The Future of an Illusion*. But I believe his negative attitude to religion and that of many of his followers is to be attributed much more to the widespread scepticism about religion in many intellectual circles during the past hundred years than to any inherent anti-religious bias in psychology. On the contrary I believe that psychology, and dynamic psychology in particular, can shed new light on what the gospel has to say about man.

The first lesson of dynamic psychology is the mysteriousness of man. It sees man as a whole of which his conscious thinking and deciding is just the tip of the iceberg. For a picture of man based on the insights of psychology we will turn not to a professional psychologist but to a man of letters.

Aldous Huxley has given a vivid description of man as psychology has taught him to understand him. 'Every human being is a conscious self, but below the threshhold of consciousness every human being is also a not-self or more precisely has five or six merging but clearly distinguishable not-selfs. There is first of all the personal home-made not-self, the not-self of habit and conditioned reflexes, the not-self of impulse repressed but still obscurely alive, the not-self of buried alive reactions to remote events and forgotten words, the not-self of fossil infancy and the festering remains of a past that refuses to die. This personal not-self is that region of the sub-conscious with which psychiatry mainly deals. Next comes the not-self which used to be called the vegetative soul or *entelechy*. This is the not-self in charge of the body – the not-self who when we wish to walk actually does the walking, the not-self who controls our breathing, our heart beat, our glandular secretions; the not-self that is prepared to digest even doughnuts; the not-self that heals wounds and brings us back to health when we have been ill. Then there is the not-self who inhabits the world from which we derive our insights and inspirations. This is the not-self who spoke to Socrates through his daimon, who dreamed the text of *Kubla Khan,* who dictated *King Lear* and the *Agamemnon* and the *Tibetan Book of the Dead,* the not-self who is responsible in all of us for every enhancement of wisdom, every sudden accession of vital or intellectual power. Beyond this world of inspiration lies the world of what Jung has called the archetypes – those great shared symbols which stand for man's deepest tendencies, his perennial conflicts and ubiquitous problems. Next comes the world of visionary experience, where a mysterious not-self lives in the midst, not of shared human symbols but of shared non-human facts – facts from which the theologians of the various religions have derived their notions of the other world, of heaven and hell. And finally, beyond all the rest, but immanent in every mental or material event, is that universal not-self, which men have called the Holy Spirit, the Atman Brahman, the Clear Light, Suchness.[7]

This long quotation must serve as a preliminary description of the iceberg of which our conscious thinking and deciding is just the tip. The christian spiritual tradition and dynamic psychology though they approach the understanding of man from different directions and with different presuppositions are united in affirming that he possesses heights and depths of which he knows very little. They also agree on the importance of self-knowledge. Indeed probably the greatest single gift that psychology can make to christian spirituality is a new set of names and tools for gaining this knowledge. Further, a brief sketch of Carl Jung's conception of the Self will help to explain the way I understand God to guide our lives. The son of a Swiss pastor, Jung was all his life concerned about religion. The importance he attached to religion was one of the factors which led to his breach with the atheist Freud after having closely collaborated with him for several years. Jung regarded what he called the God archetype, the tendency in man to acknowledge an absolute, a transcendent authority which it was dangerous to ignore, was the most fundamental of all man's tendencies. When, in a well-known television interview which he gave not long before his death, he was asked by John Freeman if he believed in God, he replied: 'I don't need to believe: I know.' He claimed to have an experience of God, of a present reality, of a presence and a pressure which it was impossible for him to deny. In speaking of the Self Jung uses a quite different terminology from that of Huxley in the above quotation. Huxley means by self the conscious person which roughly corresponds with what Freud and Jung alike call the ego. Huxley's various not-selfs would in Jung's terminology be better called non-egos or not-"I"s. Jung would regard them all as part of the Self, a term borrowed from Indian religion to which he gave a double meaning. Its first meaning is the total personality, both the conscious personality, the ego, and Huxley's other levels of personality which together comprise the unconscious. The ego is both part of the Self and its executive agent; through the thinking, planning, deciding ego the Self, the total person, makes its impact on the world. The second meaning supplementing the first and closely related to it, is the personality centre, the point of balance within the personality. The two conceptions are interdependent, for a centre implies a circle or an area of which it is the centre. Jung was aware of the pressure of the Self upon his conscious personality sometimes as a whole influencing a part, sometimes as a deep centre acting like a magnet upon the ego. Assagioli[8] is describing a similar experience, though with slightly different nuances of meaning, when he speaks of the higher centre or self to distinguish it from the lower centre, the ego.

This awareness of the Self was often accompanied, both in Jung's own experience and in that of some of his patients, by a powerful sense of the numinous and by strong religious feeling. Occasionally Jung with characteristic verbal imprecision is led to speak of the Self as God. But it is more consistent with his usual language as well as with Christian theology to understand the Self, the total personality or its centre, as a sign of God's presence, as that through which God makes his presence known to the conscious personality.

The idea of the soul's centre as the place where God is to be found is no discovery of Jung. Christian mystical writers who assume that God is present everywhere affirm that he is most surely to be found within, and many of them, Julian of Norwich, St Teresa and St John of the Cross to name only a few, understand the soul's centre to be the place of God's indwelling. I shall regard the centre as the symbol through which 'the inexhaustible fund of invention and contrivance' signals his presence to every man who has eyes to see and ears to hear.

The plan of this book is first to outline the goal and meaning of man's life as affirmed by the gospel, interpreted and worked out in practice by the christian spiritual tradition and illuminated by modern psychology. It will then seek to shed further light on life's meaning as well as to help self-understanding by looking at the stages of life – infancy and childhood, adolescence and adulthood, early and late – and reflecting on the special tasks and difficulties of each stage. It will go on to examine the means and methods by which men in the christian tradition can be helped in the pursuit of life's goal, especially the practice of prayer, and to see what light psychology can shed upon them.

1. This collection of essays by Jung is an excellent introduction to his psychology.
2. De Caussade: *Abandonment to Divine Providence*

3. Austin Farrer, *Saving Belief* (Hodder & Stoughton, 1964) p. 51.
4. Austin Farrer, op. cit. p. 43.
5. Austin Farrer, op. cit. p. 51.
6. Austin Farrer, op. cit. p. 51.
7. From an essay on *The Education of an Amphibian* in *Adonis and the Alphabet* (Bodley Head/Chatto and Windus)
8. *Psychosynthesis* (Hobbs, Dorman & Co. 1965) Chapter 1.

# 2. The Human Journey

The river is within us, the sea is all about us.
T.S. Eliot, The Dry Salvages l. 15

It will suit my purpose of anchoring the gospel firmly in the contemporary world if I begin the discussion of the meaning and goal of human life, not with the affirmations of the gospel, true though I hold them to be, but with a psychological view of man. At first sight it may seem that there is little in common between the outlook of the psychotherapist and that of the preacher of the gospel. The preacher speaks of God, of sin and repentance, of forgiveness and grace, of heaven and hell. None of these words occur in the vocabulary of the psychotherapist with the exception of forgiveness; and by forgiveness he will have in mind something different from what the preacher generally means. He will speak for example of the need a person has to forgive himself. But we must not be misled by differences of vocabulary into overlooking the profound agreement between some of the empirical discoveries of psychology and the basic truths of the gospel.

## PSYCHOLOGY AND MAN'S DESTINY

Life after death is beyond the purview of the psychotherapist who is concerned with life in this world, while the gospel speaks of eternal life, a life that goes on for ever. But the eternal life which is a major theme of St John's gospel is not simply unending life, but an enhanced quality of life, a fuller, richer, freer life which begins in this world though it is consummated in the next. The psychologist can shed a flood of meaning on the 'this world' meaning of eternal life. One of the ways the psychotherapist understands the goal of life is as the attainment of self-realization. He works on the assumption that each person has an inborn need so far as possible to realise his capacities to the full. Abraham Maslow, the American psychiatrist, for example, affirms the potential greatness of the human person. Over and above a person's biological needs and his need to get on with his fellows and cope with his environment he has an urge to affirm and by affirming to actualise his essential being. The person who learns to realise and live out his essential nature he calls the self-actualising person and he describes some of the qualities of such a person. He tends to be more integrated, more responsible, more contented, better able to relate to his fellows. In other words Maslow sees the goal of life as the making actual of your potential, the letting the seeds of character and achievement with which you are endowed germinate, grow and blossom out to the full.

Jung described the need for self-realization in terms of individuation, that is to say of the acceptance and living out by the individual of his own specific nature, the becoming more and more what he truly is, the living out of his own truth. Jung would also understand the urge to individuation as due to the pressure of the Self, whether understood as the total personality or as the personality centre, upon the conscious person to acknowledge his deep needs and to face the challenges and risks and make the decisions which will enable him to grow to his full human stature. If we are right as suggested in chapter one in seeing the centre as that through which God makes his presence known, then the magnetic pull of the centre of which Jung writes helps to bring to life the traditional doctrine that all men desire God. The most famous expression of this doctrine is that of St Augustine in his *Confessions* 'O God, thou has made us for thyself and our hearts are restless until they rest in thee'. These words which have awakened a deep response in the hearts of many a believer in the past are apt to sound unreal to the typical modern, who perceives that men appear to set their hearts on quite other goals than God: money, power, personal recognition, domestic happiness, friends or some social or political object. And though it is not hard to recognise that such goals as these however good in themselves cannot permanently satisfy, yet the idea of God seems too distant, too shadowy to satisfy either. But if we understand the desire for God as the desire to be at one with our true centre, the desire to live in accordance with the truth of our being, then this ancient doctrine is infused with new and exciting meaning. The desire to rest in God will be seen as a desire to live from our centre, to express our own truth, to be centred, integrated, a city at unity in itself.

The theologian will not be content to understand oneness with God simply in terms of personal integration, inner unity and peace. He will want to add that the desire for harmony with God must include if it is genuine the desire to be at one with our fellows. For God dwells in them as he dwells in us and is concerned for them exactly as he is concerned for us. The desire for God does not draw us away from other people but towards them. But the psychotherapist will not disagree. The various schools of dynamic psychology and psychotherapy have tended to concentrate on the self-realisation of the individual. But they all take for granted that this self-realisation can only occur in and through relationships with others. A person does not realize himself at the expense of others. If he attempts to do so he discovers that he has succeeded in developing certain elements in himself only through rejecting other equally important elements; for example he may realize his urge to power and success only by sacrificing his need for love or friendship. The theologian will want to go further, where the psychotherapist cannot follow unless he steps out of his own discipline. He will affirm that the desire for God though it includes the desire for personal integration and for oneness with our fellows is something more. For though God is actively present within us and within other people he transcends the grasp of our minds. The desire for union with God is a desire for oneness with an Unknown whom we know only dimly and in part, whom we can only approach if we do so in a spirit of reverence. But though this idea of a transcendent God who is also immanent within us and others goes beyond the range of ideas with which the psychotherapist works it does not conflict with those ideas.

The gospel takes for granted that only union with God can ultimately satisfy the human heart. As we have seen it is able to welcome the new insight of empirical psychology into the needs and urges of man's nature as bringing fresh evidence to support and enrich its understanding of the human condition. Christian writers have used a very different style from that of the contemporary psychologist in describing the meaning and goal of man's life. From the time when Jesus taught by parables right up to the present day they have resorted to metaphor, symbol and story. One of the commonest metaphors they have used is that of the journey. A journey through space is a natural metaphor for the passage through time. St Bernard in the eleventh century remarked that man journeys to God not by the steps of his feet but by the turning of his heart; the Godward journey is a growth towards an increasing union with God. Three centuries later Walter Hilton, the English mystical writer, described the life of a contemplative as that of a pilgrim seeking Jerusalem, his heart and mind and all his energies bent on attaining to the vision of Jesus in the city of peace, a vivid new statement of St Augustine's desire to rest in God. But much the best known use of this metaphor in the English language is that of the seventeenth century John Bunyan's *Pilgrim's Progress*.

The pilgrimage which Bunyan describes is the story of the turning of a man's heart and mind despite many vicissitudes to embrace more and more wholeheartedly God and salvation. It is hope together with hope's companion fear that sets Christian off on his journey from the City of Destruction to the Celestial City. The indispensable need of hope is brought out powerfully in the pilgrim's struggle with discouragement and despair. At the very outset of his pilgrimage Christian falls into the Slough of Despond. Again, far on in the journey in one of its most exciting incidents Bunyan tells of the capture of Christian and his young companion Hopeful by Giant Despair and their imprisonment in one of the dungeons of Doubting Castle, until they remember that they carry in their breasts a key called promise which can open all locks, and so they make their escape. The psychotherapist will agree that hope and effort are both needed if a person is to realize himself, to live out his own truth. The gospel which declares God's measureless love for mankind and his promise of eternal life for all who will pay the price of accepting it provides an incentive for hope which psychology is not competent to give. Psychology in return can do much to free christians from their perennial temptation to escape into fantasy, their temptation to make the hope of heaven hereafter an excuse for not working to make this world more heavenly, for not trying to walk with God, to be at one with God in the present, for not battling to make this world a better and a juster one. For the psychotherapist works with people who suffer from deep and discouraging frustration, people who are obsessed with life's impossibilities; and one of his tasks is to help awaken a realistic hope. He knows that the hope for something unrealisable, the dream of something that cannot possibly happen, is an ingredient in the despair that paralyses effort. His task is to encourage them to abandon wishful thinking and begin to imagine real possibilities, to imagine the kind of practical achievement which will rouse their energy and move them to act. The christian pastor can learn from the experience of the psychotherapist to scrutinize motives. The hope of heaven has provided and ought to provide the powerful incentive to commitment to the present, for action in the here and now is the road to heaven. But this hope has sometimes been a source of energy-sapping fantasy.[1]

## PSYCHOLOGY AND SIN

Another service which psychology can render to christian spirituality is to help liberate it from an undue emphasis on human sin and guilt. The psychotherapist knows from experience the large number of men and women in whom a morbid sense of guilt, totally out of proportion to any actual misdeed, is a major factor in mental breakdown. This overemphasis casts a shadow over *Pilgrim's Progress* and many other christian writings. It implies a doctrine of God's wrath, expressed in condemning men and women to eternal torment, at variance with the gospel of his love and compassion. It is

true that the doctrine of divine love and compassion is there,
and the emphasis on man's sin and guilt is partly designed to
heighten the generosity and mercy of God in sending his Son
at great cost to earn forgiveness for man and reconcile him to
God. Christian sets out from the City of Destruction to the
Celestial City with a burden on his back. No effort of his own
and no advice from others can free him from it. It drops off of
its own accord as he stands looking intently at a wayside
crucifix. The incident is movingly described, and vividly
portrays God's love and compassion. But God's vindictive
wrath is also present in the background in unresolved con-
tradiction to the divine mercy.

This stress on man's sin and guilt is in striking contrast to
the gospel and the teaching of Jesus. The gospel does indeed
assume without argument that there is something seriously the
matter with men and the way men live. But the emphasis of
Jesus, unlike the traditional teaching we have been considering, is on man's weakness and need, his inability to help
himself, rather than on his wickedness. He is like a lost sheep
needing a shepherd to find him and bring him home. He is like
a sick man in need of a doctor. He is in the grip of demonic
powers and needs to be set free. The gospel in brief is the good
news that God cares infinitely for man; that he will set free and
make whole all who seek freedom and health from him, all
who will commit themselves to his Kingdom. Jesus himself is
the sign of God's love and the agent through which God's
blessings are brought to man. The doctrine of God's wrath
and the doctrine of hell do indeed find a place in the teaching
of Jesus, but with another emphasis than what we find in
*Pilgrim's Progress.* Jesus' own illustration of the sick man and
the doctor is a pointer to the way we are to understand God's
wrath. It is because God loves men and women that he is un-
alterably hostile to what is destroying them, just as a doctor
may be said to wage war against the cancer that is killing his
patient.

This view of the sinner as really a sick man is highly
congenial to psychology. But does it weaken the sense of the
reality of evil and man's responsibility for his actions? It need
not weaken our perception of evil. We can recognise that
cruelty and arrogance, treachery, sloth and cowardice are

thoroughly bad even though, taught by psychology, we are able to discern behind the black deed or the disastrous inaction a frightened man or woman, hag-ridden by infantile cravings for power or sadistic impulses or fear of rejection. This realisation of the irrational compulsions by which men can be driven need not lead us to condone their actions though it will make us less inclined to blame the men themselves. This will bring us close to the teaching of Jesus who insists that we must not condemn others if we wish to escape condemnation ourselves. But will not this refusal to condemn wrongdoers encourage utter irresponsibility? It does not do so in the teaching of Jesus. The thrust of his words is not against the wickedness of sin but its folly. Like the driving instructor who does not tell his pupil that it is wicked to drive on the wrong side of the road but that it will most probably prove fatal, so Jesus affirms that sin is self-destructive, it leads to death.

No honest reading of the gospels can eliminate from them Jesus' teaching about hell. He uses the imagery familiar to his hearers to warn them of the danger of trifling with salvation. The imagery is mainly of exclusion or destruction; and as with all imagery it is possible to read into it a variety of meanings. It is only reasonable however to interpret it in the light of Jesus' insistence on God's measureless love and his desire for the salvation of all men. The doctrine of hell points to the weakness of omnipotent Love. Men must choose salvation, they cannot be forced into it nor will it come about by accident. But to suppose, as has been thought, that God would punish men with unending torture is to read into the imagery of the gospels a meaning which contradicts reason as well as all that we know of Jesus's teaching about God. To speculate about the life to come is to guess in the dark. But because we cannot altogether keep our minds off it I will sum up this discussion of hell with two brief quotations from Austin Farrer. 'There seem to be only two credible reasons for consigning souls to flame; either for remedial discipline or for extirpation.'[2] 'Men whose moral misery is disguised from them by comfort, pride or success, will find themselves after death a prey to that flame which can surely be nothing but the scorching truth.'[3]

The many christian teachers and writers who have tried to

inculcate a sense of the wickedness of sin and the guilt of man were supported in their endeavours by beliefs connected with the story of Adam and Eve in Eden. The story was understood as literal history; Adam and Eve were thought to have been created in a state of sinless perfection at peace with God and their own natural environment, to have deliberately disobeyed the express command of God, to have lost their innocence and to have been excluded from the bliss of Eden. Further man not only suffered the estrangement from God and the tendency to evil which were believed to be the consequence of Adam's sin but also shared Adam's guilt and so were right to feel guilty. What we know of man's descent from animal ancestors, of the long struggle for survival of the earliest men, and the very slow attainment of a position of dominance in the animal kingdom, makes it very difficult to fit anything like the Eden story into an account of man's origins. It is better to understand the Eden story as telling timeless truths about man as he is rather than as providing factual information about the dawn of history. The innocence of Adam and Eve in the garden speaks of the innocence of childhood before it has acquired the knowledge of good and evil; the innocence of childhood as looked back upon by adults who remember the carefree days of spontaneity and irresponsibility and forget the frustrations and bleak moods of their early years. The perfection of Adam as understood by traditional theology is an intuition of the perfection of which he is capable, it is a dream in man's mind beckoning him towards a future in which it might be realised. John Hick has suggested that man exists at a distance from God's goal for him, not because he has fallen from that goal but because he has yet to arrive at it.[4] Instead of having been created perfect, man is in the making. Under the invisible pressure of 'the inexhaustible power for good and the inexhaustible fund of invention and contrivance' he is being persuaded towards becoming by his own decisions and actions the man he is designed to be. Sin then is a clinging to the past, a reluctance to take the apparent risk of pressing on to his full human destiny; it is a failure of hope.

Whether we think of man's present condition as a degeneration from a primitive state of innocence or perfection or as a half-way stage on the road to becoming fully human there is certainly something wrong with man as he is. The theologian sees him as estranged from God, at loggerheads with his fellows and within himself a house divided. If we are right in taking the Jungian concept of the Self, in its dual character as both the total personality and the personality centre, as the key to an understanding of the way God acts upon us and makes himself known to us, then it will follow inevitably that being estranged from God will mean being unaware of and out of touch with the heights and depths of our personality; it will mean being estranged from our centre and unable to live our own truth. The sickness and the lostness of man which the gospels describe is a condition in which he is carried away by unconscious fears and desires, is deaf to the promptings of an intuitive wisdom, rejects forces within himself making for health and healing, and finds the spring of life poisoned. Out of touch with his true centre, 'the heart's heart', man is driven by an innate need to find another centre, an absolute to give order and direction to his life; he is liable to find himself compulsively attached to some cause or object which takes the place of his true centre. He is driven to give absolute or at least greatly exaggerated value to some objective of real but only limited value, some false centre such as personal ambition, sexual satisfaction, wealth, fame, popularity, or perhaps some concrete object such as a family, party or nation. In a book published before the war,[5] in which he described the rise of the Nazis to power in Germany Peter Drucker wrote of a street scene he had witnessed. A speaker addressing a crowd of cheering Germans was saying 'We don't want lower bread prices, we don't want higher bread prices, we don't want unchanged bread prices, what we want is National Socialist bread prices.' What the man was saying with his crazy rhetoric was that the price of bread was purely secondary. What mattered was that the price of bread and every other detail of the nation's political and economic life should be settled by the party and its leader, Adolf Hitler. He was apppealing to the need for an absolute, a centre of authority, something men could put their whole trust in. Perhaps the only way to avoid attaching ourselves to some false centre, whether a cause, a person or some aspect of ourselves is to discover and submit to the authority of our true centre, the place where God makes his presence and purpose for us known.

To be attached to a false centre inevitably leads to division within the personality, for such a centre can only claim the allegiance of part of a person. St Paul has described this state of inner division, the conflict between his conscious aim and ideal, what he calls the law of his mind, and the urges from within, that contradict his ideals and bring them to nothing, what he calls the law of sin. 'The good that I would, that I do not; the evil that I would not, that I do.'[6] Somehow, through Jesus Christ, and through trusting himself to him he found himself at peace, renewed, set free, remade. He found himself in touch with his true centre, acknowledging its authority over his life; he found himself at one with God. Can psychology help to make this experience unquestionably authentic to St Paul intelligible to the typical man of the twentieth century? Plenty of christians today live by relying on the grace of Christ without attempting to understand it. They are apt to be suspicious lest psychology attempt to explain away an experience which they know to be real. But psychology steps right out of its province if it tries to explain an experience of the divine in purely human terms. There is however a human element in every experience of God, and a psychology that can shed light on this human element should strengthen not weaken our grasp of the spiritual reality experienced.

## PSYCHOLOGY AND CONVERSION

Perhaps Jung's concept of the reconciling symbol can illuminate St Paul's experience of conversion. A symbol is much more than a sign pointing to something known. It can be described as the best available statement of an unknown reality. A living symbol might be explained as a powerful image, focusing the imagination, releasing the emotions, moving to action. A symbol moves us, shifts our centre of awareness, it speaks to our depths and changes our values; it does something to us. The simplest illustration of the effect of a symbol is falling in love. When Jack falls in love with Jill the image of Jill focuses Jack's imagination, releases his emotions, moves him to action: it changes him. Jack feels himself a different person; the image of Jill has become the focus of emotions and energies of which he did not know himself to be capable. Jung calls the living symbol a psychological machine which transforms energy locked up in the unconscious into energy available for action, like the giant turbines which turn the waters of Niagara into electricity to provide light and heat to half a million homes.

The power of religion to change the lives of its adherents derives from its symbols which speak to man's depths and release the psychic energy that sleeps there, waiting for the right summons to awaken it and call it into action. The central christian symbol is that of Jesus Christ himself. He is more than just a symbol, but it is because he is able to be for us a living symbol that he can transform our lives. The transforming symbol for St Paul was the crucified and risen Messiah who met with him on the road to Damascus. That powerful image brought together within a single focus the opposing forces warring within him; his devotion to the law as the expression of the will of the all-righteous God of Israel and the ambitions and lusts of the natural man were drawn into harmony by the symbol of the Crucified. That the Son of the most High should identify himself with mankind in its estrangement to the point of dying in dishonour on the cross filled him with amazement and wonder. 'He who knew no sin became sin for us.'[7] 'He loved me and gave himself for me.'[8] An immense capacity for love and self-sacrifice was released in the new Paul. Without abandoning the moral ideal embodied in the jewish law with which he had grown up he found himself impelled by a power transcending the law and teaching him the higher law of love. 'Owe no man anything but to love one another; for love is the fulfilling of the law.'[9]

To be fully effective a symbol must act as a link between two worlds. It must belong in some sense to the world of every day, the world of getting a living, of marriage and family life and friendship, of politics and established religion. But it must also belong to the unconscious depths hidden below the surface of men's lives, to the world of dream and ancient myth and buried wisdom, of the psychic and the uncanny. It must be a

bridge with firm foundations on both sides of the river it spans.
One reason why Christianity has lost ground in the Western
world is that many of its once living and powerful symbols
appear to have died or to be dying because they seem out of
place in the secularized culture of the twentieth century. They
seem to have a tenuous and insubstantial character by contrast with the bustling, inescapable world of every day. The
task of repairing the bridge between the secular world and the
deep truths of the gospel requires the cooperation of many
builders: theologians and philosophers, preachers and
evangelists, poets, artists and men of prayer. But perhaps no
science will be more important in this task of reconstruction,
just because she is a child of our times, than psychology.

The voice that spoke to Saul on the road to Damascus was
able to change the whole aim and direction of his life, not only
because it expressed the love and the demand of the all-holy
God whom from his childhood he had worshipped but because
that love and demand had been declared not in vision or story
but in the broad daylight of recent history. The visions of the
prophets and the ancient, symbolic ritual of sacrifice had been
made alive and contemporary by what took place on a recent
Friday outside the walls of Jerusalem. Those who accept the
ideas of Jung will be inclined to relate the rapid growth of
Christianity to its fulfilment of one of the ancient myths which
goes back so far as we know to the dawn of history, the myth of
the dying and rising God. The power and persistence of the
myth is far greater than can be accounted for only by the cycle
of the seasons and the annual spring flooding of the Nile in
Egypt and of the Tigris and Euphrates in Mesopotamia. Its
power is due to its correspondence with a deep truth of
human nature. The myth embodies the truth that an old ideal
must die before a new ideal can be born, that the old ruling
principle, the old king, must die before the new king can come
to the throne, that something beautiful and precious must be
sacrificed before new life can be born, that we must lose our
lives if we would save them. These truths were hinted at in the
stories of the dying and rising gods of the ancient world; but
the stories belonged to the world of dream and fantasy not to
that of every day. They woke echoes in men's minds of
sacrifice being the law of life and of rebirth through suffering

but they lacked power. But the life, death and resurrection of Jesus took place on the stage of history, the vigorous and expanding christian church bore powerful and contemporary witness to it. The crucified and risen Jesus, alive and active in his disciples became a bridge between the everyday life of the Roman Empire and the mysterious depths of the men of that world.[10]

St Paul understands the christian life as one of identification with the crucified and risen Messiah. This is the primary meaning of both baptism and the eucharist. Sometimes he speaks of Christ as being in the christian, sometimes of the christian as being in Christ. His theology of Messiah is new-minted out of experience and it is not to be expected that it should be wholly self-consistent. Though he does not call Christ God in so many words, yet the way he speaks of him implies his godhead or his unique oneness with God. Jung, explaining the christian experience in terms of his own psychology, speaks of Christ, in a phrase that at first sounds shocking to christian ears, as a symbol of the Self. But if we understand the Self to signify either the total personality or the personality centre through which God makes himself known to us the phrase takes on new meaning. Christ is then seen as the key that opens the door not only to the mystery of our own being but to the immensely greater mystery of the being of God and of his purpose for us.

Living the christian life seriously means working out in practice the meaning of identification with Christ. This has been understood in many ways by christians in the past. It seems important today to realize that to be one with Christ means to be at one with one's own centre. I believe this truth, not always apparent at the outset of the christian journey becomes increasingly clear as the journey progresses. A man comes to realize that it is from within, from the centre of his being that he finds the help he needs. In perplexity he turns to the centre for guidance, in weakness he turns to the centre for strength. This is how Christ guides and strengthens him. He will indeed help and direct him from outside as well. He addresses a man through his brother, through the community of faith to which he belongs, through every soul he meets. He speaks also through the Scriptures, through the wisdom of the past enshrined in tradition, through teachers and prophets of today. But the help and direction that comes from outside is only fully assimilated and made genuinely his own when it is related to the centre within. In the centre dwells the christian's pillar of fire by night and pillar of cloud by day. It is the focus of God's action and the sanctuary where he dwells.

According to one school within the christian spiritual tradition an essential part of the christian's task of bringing his life into harmony with Christ is the struggle to gain self-knowledge. Without benefit of Freud or Jung they discovered empirically some of the truths that modern dynamic psychology has brought to light. They knew that a person may easily be unaware or only partly aware of ambitions and lusts, of loves and hates, of hopes and fears which, far more than he realizes dictate his plans and actions. If he is to come to know God who dwells within him, he must come to know the hidden emotions, the secret passions, which surround the Centre and which he must help to bring under its sway. 'Swink and sweat' in all that thou can'st and mayest,' writes the anonymous fourteenth century author of *The Cloud of Unknowing*,' for to get thee a true knowing and feeling of thyself as thou art. And then, I trow, soon after that thou wilt get thee a true knowing and feeling of God as he is.'[11] It is no theoretical knowledge which this medieval author is alluding to but a real awareness of the hidden motives, the unconscious dynamism within a man.

The work of finding our true centre and of bringing the whole personality into harmony with it and with God who guides us through it is the work of a lifetime. There are stages in the journey, and tasks to be accomplished and obstacles to be surmounted at each stage. Further the failure to fulfil the tasks or overcome the difficulties of an early stage can haunt and hinder a person later on, as the schoolboy's failure to master the elementary grammar of a subject will sap his confidence and spoil his efforts at a more advanced level. For the experiences of infancy, childhood, and adolescence, though largely or even totally forgotten, live on into middle life and old age in the form of buried fears and imprisoned rage, which still exercise a hidden influence, as well as habits and tendencies begun in answer to some crisis in the past and continuing through the strength of habit. Self-knowledge and the integration which this makes possible come partly through recalling and becoming reconciled with the past. To assist the work of recall the next three chapters will consider the special tasks and difficulties of the successive stages of life, beginning with the years of infancy and childhood. [12]

1. *Images of Hope* by W.F. Lynch S.J. (Mentor Omega, 1965) is a useful study, psychological and theological, of hope.
2. *Saving Belief.* p. 153.
3. Op. cit. p. 153.
4. *Evil and the God of Love.* Pt. 4 Ch.14. (Macmillan 1966) pp. 316–327
5. *The End of Economic Man* (Heinemann. 1939)
6. Rom. 7.19.
7. 2 Cor. 5, 21.
8. Gal. 2, 20.
9. Rom. 13. 8
10. See Victor White. *God and the Unconscious.* Chap.12. The Dying God.
11. *The Cloud of Unknowing.* Chapt. 14.
12. For a fuller treatment of Jung's idea of the Self as illuminating the experience of God, see my *Depth Psychology and Religious Belief* (Mirfield Publications, 1972) Chapter 2.

# 3.  The Father of the Man

Quick, said the bird, find them, find them,
Round the corner. Through the first gate,
Into our first world, shall we follow
The deception of the thrush? Into our first world?
                           T.S. Eliot, *Burnt Norton* ll. 19 – 22


It is no part of my aim in this chapter on the tasks and
difficulties of infancy and childhood to advise parents how to
bring up their children. Its chief purpose is to help adults who
may or may not be parents to become more conscious of the unsolved problems of their own childhood and so to grow in the
self-awareness which is an essential preliminary to becoming
centred and integrated. The experience of childhood, most of it
now wrapt in oblivion, is a hidden ever-present influence within
us. Eric Berne in his *Transactional Analysis in Psychotherapy*,[1] better known for his book, *The Games People Play*,[2] offers a simple
key to the understanding of the motives that determine or
colour behaviour. In each person there are, as it were, three
principles of action, the adult, the parent and the child. It is as if
in addition to our rational adult selves there lived within us two
sub-personalities, either of which might from time to time dictate our words and actions: the child that we once were and
another sub-personality, not our actual parents but an inner
authority figure built up from our childhood impression of our
parents together with their dos and don'ts. It is easy to criticize
this scheme as over-simple, but the light it sheds on behaviour is

an indication that it contains much truth. It is clearly a development of Freud's trinity of ego, superego and id. In its personification of elements within the personality it resembles Jung's theory of archetypes. It gives added emphasis to the importance of coming to terms with the past if we are to respond creatively to the present.


## THE NEEDS AND PROBLEMS OF INFANCY

Facing the past is also important if we wish to grasp the reality of God's action within us. One of the aims of this book is to explore the human story from the standpoint of christian belief, which means to view it in the context of God's active presence in it from beginning to end. The God who 'makes us make ourselves' brings us into the world through the agency of parents. God's creative will operates through immensely powerful biological instincts which like a mighty river carry the human race on towards its destiny. Individual men and women can steer a course upon this river, but they are powerless to arrest its flow. Parents are God's agents in the care and nurture of their children, agents who knowingly or unknowingly, wisely or unwisely cooperate with him. They are enabled to do this partly by inborn instinct and intuition, partly through the traditional wisdom handed down by grandmothers and brought up to date by doctors and child experts, partly by their own practical intelligence and ingenuity.

The experts are agreed on the all-importance for a person's subsequent life of the earliest years of childhood. During that critical period an emotional attitude to the world, as for example a welcoming or a dangerous or in some cases an actively hostile place, begins to develop which may persist through life; first impressions here are apt to be decisive. But a curtain of oblivion hangs in our minds screening those initial years from memory's scrutiny, a curtain which can only partially and with difficulty be drawn aside. This curtain hides from us a period of strong emotion and vivid fantasy life. The infant is at the mercy of what looks like a chaos of intensely powerful emotions, which seem to take possession of him like a demon. Terror and rage, possessive love, jealousy and hate, rapturous bliss, deep content and fascinated curiosity, joy and despair sometimes succeed one another in rapid succession. His great needs are food at regular intervals, care for his bodily comfort and cleanliness, protection from danger, and love; and when these are all available at the right time the infant's life may be relatively tranquil. But at the best of times there is bound to be much frustration. He cannot speak and tell about the tiger of hunger that is gnawing at his inside or the sharp pain caused by excessive wind or the terror caused by the bark of a dangerous looking dog or the sudden stab of a spark from the fire. He is totally dependent on the care and understanding of others, who will have other things to do besides looking after him, who may be suddenly called away, who may fall ill and even die. At this early stage the infant's fantasy life is strong. Indeed there is a very thin line between dream, fantasy and waking, and it is difficult for the infant to distinguish between fantasy and what to us is the real world. The fantasies express and in some measure compensate for unsatisfied needs. It is probable that fantasies of fighting and murder help to appease his towering rages, that fantasies of safety help to calm his fears and fantasies of being loved his loneliness, that fantasies of omnipotence help to solace his helplessness. This fantasy of omnipotence, the feeling of being like God, secure from all mishap and able to command instant obedience, is peculiarly seductive. It is also sometimes fostered by the infant's one weapon. Few adults can listen unmoved to the piteous wailing of an infant and in happy circumstances the baby's cry brings the swift comfort of being picked up in strong and gentle arms.

The fantasy life of infants is fed by the fairy stories that he learns as he grows older. He is able to identify with the characters in the story both bad and good, with Little Red Riding Hood and also in horror with the wolf that devours her. Such stories help him to come to terms with his own fears and his own aggression. For fantasy is not only a way of escape from reality, it can also be a means of facing and mastering reality. The images and symbols of fantasy seem to be the only means by which the conscious mind can catch and harness the powerful energies of the unconscious. Play, which is an acting out of fantasy in ritual form, is important in the life of children in

helping them to integrate strong inner urges with their relationships with their family and their friends. In the game of
hide and seek the child enjoys the thrill and suspense of being
in turn both hunter and hunted. In play children learn to get
on with their peers, their aggression is ritualised. This is also
true of animal play. 'Play even amongst animals is ritualised.
In play motor patterns which are used "seriously" in other
contexts where they would be biologically useful are used in
incomplete, exaggerated or "pretend" forms. Fight and flight
patterns, for example, are constantly employed in this way.'[3]
'It seems highly likely that one biological function of play is to
teach young animals to ritualise their primitive impulses of
aggression in such a way that they can fit into a social group,
whilst at the same time preserving their capabilities for serious
fight in reality should the occasion call for it.'[4] What is true of
the young animal is also true of young and growing human
animals.

One of the ways in which the powerful emotions of fear and
aggression are brought out into the open and civilised is
through games. Another way is through drawing and painting.
With the help of pencil or paintbrush children are sometimes
able to objectify, to contemplate as something outside themselves, the oppressive nightmare fears of infancy. Frances
Wickes quotes this incident which a school teacher observed
and recorded. 'A little boy had kept himself apart from all the
activities in the classroom, but watched with interest the
children who were painting. One day he too began to paint. His
pictures were of dark, shadowy monsters. They were "The
terrible Things in the House at Night", "the terrible Things
under the Sea", "the terrible Things outside the Window."
One day he chose gay colours, green and yellow and blue.
When someone remarked on the change he said casually.
"Oh! the terrible things are gone. I have put them all in the
pictures." By painting his terrors the child gave them shape
and objectivity, he put them outside himself where he could
not only look at them but share them with others. In this way
he broke their magic spell over him. The trolls that are deadly
in the dark are turned to stone in the daylight.

We have moved on from the world of infancy, of nightmare
fantasy and of helpless dependence on others to a stage when
the child is taking his first steps in independence. But we must

turn back in order to recall our first and greatest resource in
babyhood, the loving care of mother. During this period of
emotional storm and stress the infant needs much attention to
his purely bodily needs. But over and above these he has a
desperate need for a love which is grasped very much in the
physical terms of being hugged and held and caressed. Without this physically expressed love, which mothers normally
delight to give, it has been discovered from the experience of
homes for motherless babies, the infant will wilt and die. 'Towards the end of the Second World War an American paedia-
trician, Margaret Ribble, carried out a very significant experiment. Having noticed that the infants in a home for motherless babies were deprived and sickly, despite good physical
care and feeding, she arranged that a group of them should be
given special treatment: every day, for half an hour, a nurse
was to take each baby and 'mother' it, rocking it in her arms
and cuddling and stroking it. The results were dramatic: the
babies brightened up and began to put on weight. Formerly
many of them had had breathing difficulties; these now disappeared. The mortality rate declined sharply.' [6]'It is impossible to exaggerate the importance of mother, or of some
mother surrogate, during the early months of an infant's life.
As Dr Dominian has written. 'All feelings are initiated in the
heavenly experience of oneness between the young infant and
its mother in which the feelings of recognition, acceptance and
tenderness are exchanged unconditionally through looks,
caresses and words. These needs remain permanently in
human beings and psychoanalysts work continuously with
persons who have never experienced these feelings adequately
and are handicapped in innumerable ways either in expressing or receiving them.' [7] The infant's first experience of God is
mediated normally through his mother. The concept 'God'
will mean nothing to him for a long time. But he is aware of a
caring, a warmth and a tenderness to which he surrenders
himself in trust. Out of this seed of infant trust can grow the
strong reliance of an adult on his Creator and Redeemer. As
Dominian writes again; 'Faith, man's response to God, requires the quality of trust, which is a feeling engendered in the
earliest period of life. God is reached through our parents, not
only in the traditional sense of agents who teach us the rudi-

ments of faith but as the living springs providing us with the prototypes of the meaning of God, the source of infinite trust.' [8]

## THE INFANT ROOTS OF SOME PERSONALITY DISORDERS

Some child experts speak about two kinds of love in particular as what the growing infant needs. First and foremost is the comforting, all-accepting love of mother, the love that envelopes and protects him however naughty or trying he may be. Sometimes, it is said, a small child is deliberately disobedient, unconsciously prompted to it in order to satisfy a doubt, to make quite certain that he is loved despite the worst that he can do. Perhaps nothing is so important to a child as the certainty that he is loved for himself and that therefore he must be fundamentally lovable. But once this certainty has been sufficiently established another kind of love is needed, the conditional love that makes demands, the love that reproves naughtiness, that insists that we must behave ourselves if we are to be approved. For in addition to the basic assurance that he is loved for himself, he needs the demanding, disciplining love of father, which gives him the incentive to grow out of childish ways. This bracing, disciplining love, whether in fact it is exercised by father or mother, gives the child a sense of security. For he cannot unaided control the violent and reckless impulses that take hold of him and may lead him into hurting his friends or destroying his possessions; and he is secretly glad that there is an authority that will check him and keep him within bounds. Nor does he long resent punishment when he feels there is love behind it. When a child has received enough of both these kinds of caring, neither too little nor too much, he is likely to grow up with a sense of security, relatively free from anxiety. Perhaps most children, despite parental shortcomings do get sufficient of these two kinds of love. But it is worth noting what is liable to happen when things have gone seriously wrong.

The child who didn't have sufficient mothering is likely to go through life looking for the comforting, consoling love that as a child he never enjoyed or thought he didn't. In all sorts of relationships he will be secretly looking for someone to mother him. He or she is likely to lose many friends by making excessive demands on their time or affection. The boy who didn't get the loving discipline he needed is liable to grow up with a craving for some kind of external authority, for something that will take the strain off his conscience by telling him exactly what he should do. Authority and discipline would spell for him security. Not so for the boy or girl who had too much discipline when young. He is likely to grow up a rebel against all authority. For him authority will stand for oppression. Equally the boy or girl who had too much caring, perhaps from a possessively affectionate mother, is liable to grow up with a revulsion against all close intimacy and affection.

Looking at these two kinds of parental love from the standpoint of Christian belief I see them as pointing to two qualities of the love of God who has made man in his own image. There is first the all embracing love of the Creator who delights in all his creatures, the good and the bad, the wise and the foolish, the rich and the poor, the lot. But there is also the demanding love which is not content with us as we are, that pricks and prods and persuades us, through our nature and needs and the pressures of the world in which we find ourselves, into choosing and deciding and doing the things which will enable us to grow to our full human stature and into an intimate relationship with himself. This dual love of the Creator acts not only through parents and others but also from the centre of our being, fostering the growth both of a sense of security and of conscience.

Before going on to consider some of the positive qualities that a child needs to acquire I want to take a further look at some of the things that can go wrong and may have gone wrong with us. The study of the psychology of the mentally ill has brought to light characteristics of normal people by highlighting them in the exaggerated form they take in mental breakdown. Sometimes a child deprived at an early age of his mother, perhaps through illness or death, develops a basic mistrust of people. He was so severely wounded by the loss of his mother that he dare not let himself depend on anyone for the future. This is not, of course, a thought out policy but a quasi-instinctive habit, which makes either loving or being loved an anxiety provoking risk. He tends to be on the defensive, not only against those who seem antagonistic to him but equally against any who seek intimacy. Because personal relations are what give meaning to life, the world will seem to him empty, grey and meaningless. Indeed, sometimes the world seems positively hostile and his fellows take on the guise of enemies. This is typical of the so-called schizoid personality, who strikes us as cold, detached, bloodless. His lonely isolated attitude is not his fault but the unhappy consequence of cruel deprivation at a time when he was too young to protect himself from its effects. This is an extreme instance of what many have experienced in mild form.

Another kind of mental affliction is depression, not the occasional mood but the paralysing illness. This is caused by deprivation of love at a later stage of development than that which led to the schizoid condition just described. By the age of six months an immensely powerful emotional bond is normally formed attaching the baby to its mother. If after the formation of this bond the infant is deprived for long of his mother's presence, he becomes anxious, sorrowful, angry and finally lapses into despair. Unlike the schizoid who is detached and isolated he craves for the love which having once experienced he cannot do without. He is afraid of other people, not like the schizoid who fears lest his defensive wall of isolation be breached, but because he dreads the loss of their approval. He is inhibited by fear from expressing the anger that sometimes wells up in him, and if this should explode he blames himself with bitter self reproach.

My final example of emotional disorder originating in childhood is that of the obsessional character, which shows itself in a person's compulsive need to exercise control both of his own behaviour and of his environment. The obsessional's anxiety compels him to check and recheck whether he did indeed bolt the front door at night or switch off the electric heater or lock the safe, even though he really knows that he was careful to do all these things. He is also apt to be disgusted by dirt and worried by untidiness, so that he is continually driven to wash his hands unnecessarily just in case they are not clean and is unable to rest and relax if papers are in disorder on his desk or a chair or picture is out of alignment. Commenting on the obsessional's dislike of dirt Anthony Storr remarks 'the obsessional's habitual disgust with bodily functions, especially with those of excretion, entirely bears out Freud's contention that the origin of obsessionality is connected with the training of the child to order and control its excretory functions.'⁹ Further a tendency in a child to over-anxiety is strengthened by too much insistence by parents upon the externals of good behaviour, cleanliness, tidiness, punctuality and politeness, all good things in themselves, which may cause sensitive children to be afraid to act spontaneously, and to suppress what they really feel and really like lest they should lose the approval of their parents.

It is difficult to write about the various personality disorders which have their roots in childhood without appearing to blame parents for what has gone wrong. This in the great majority of cases would be unjust. Often mistakes are made because parents are under pressure from prevalent misconceptions about the right way to bring up children. Also there is an inherited as well as an environmental factor in most mental disorders. Infants vary enormously. Three children in a family are treated and cared for by their parents in very much the same way; one of them develops marked schizoid characteristics, the other two grow up perfectly normal. This does not mean that the home environment is unimportant. Rather it points to the fact that one child may need ten times as much mothering as another. This need for special mothering even when it is fully recognised, may be difficult if not impossible to give. And further, should it be possible to provide the extra mothering needed, it is likely to appear as gross favouritism to the other brothers and sisters, who like the brothers of Joseph may try to take it out on the favourite.

Many people will find it impossible to think about the mishaps of infancy and childhood and the unintended and often unrealized pain inflicted on them by grown ups without being reminded of their own wounds of long ago. Is there any use in recalling past hurts, or trying to relive in memory times of loneliness, moods of anger or sulkiness, of fury at punishment, the blow of disappointment or the bitter pain of feeling unwanted or unloved? Not if it leads simply to recrimination against parents or to envy of those apparently more fortunate. But for myself I have found that recalling past pain brings with it a sense of peace, of greater wholeness, of regaining contact with a lost part of myself. I find this to be true, even though my memory does not reach back to the very early years of childhood, except to a few fleeting and disconnected mental pictures, none of which are painful. Summoning times of loneliness or humiliation at the age of seven into the light of my adult comprehension seems to effect a kind of healing. It is as though the child that grieved years ago is still present within me and by attending to him with compassion I can bring him solace and comfort. I see this looking back with compassion as a way of cooperating with God who addresses me through the whole of what I am and invites me to live out my whole truth. Those who believe in the presence and power of Christ can be helped in this cooperation by what has been called faith-imagination. A person recalls, for example, a room in which as a child he had often felt very lonely. He then pictures Christ entering the room, addressing him by name, assuring him of his continual presence and love, perhaps putting his arm round him. This can be a symbolic and therefore powerful representation of two realities, that of a past experience partly active in the present and that of the living Christ.

## THE TASKS OF CHILDHOOD

We have looked at some of the things that can go wrong in infancy and childhood. Fortunately, however, things do not always go wrong and I turn now to the qualities desirable in children, the qualities that will enable them to respond positively to the opportunities and challenges that will meet them later. Erik Erikson shall be our guide and we will look one by one at the four virtues or strengths that he names as the most important in children.[10] The first of these strengths is *hope*, which Erikson defines as 'the enduring belief in the attainability of fervent wishes, in spite of the dark urges and rages that mark the beginning of existence'. The infant contains a tumult of desires: for food, warmth, protection, for being held and cuddled and for the other marks of love. His wants are bound to be thwarted sometimes, but if they are met on the whole then he begins to adopt a hopeful attitude to life. The world despite its occasional rebuffs is a kind, welcoming place and its obstacles not insurmountable. This is one of the most precious gifts that wise parental love confers on children and the lack of it is one of the greatest handicaps. The foundation of the grown up attitude of hopefulness that enables men and women to face difficulty and danger undismayed is laid in infancy. The second of Erikson's strengths of childhood is *will*, which he defines as 'the unbroken determination to exercise free choice as well as self-restraint, in spite of the unavoidable experience of shame and doubt in infancy'. This development of will, the power to make a firm choice, belongs to a slightly later stage in the child's growth. All sorts of experiences can undermine a child's confidence. He makes a remark in all seriousness which is greeted with a burst of laughter and he is filled with shame. Fear of ridicule or blame may deter a child from making known his real wishes and instead he chooses what he thinks his parents would like him to choose. However, all being well, he learns to choose and decide what he wants and not what others may wish for him. Of course he will have learnt that not all he would like is possible and to modify his choices to conform to what his parents can afford or other people can reasonably be expected to tolerate. But in learning to choose one thing and refuse another he is taking the first step towards proper independence.

The third of Erikson's strengths of childhood is *purpose* which he defines as 'the courage to envisage and pursue valued goals, uninhibited by the defeat of infantile fantasies and by guilt and the foiling fear of punishment'. This plainly marks a step further than will, the power to make a firm choice, for it assumes the ability to look ahead and the power to persevere in a chosen direction. The small child learns largely by imitation, but he can easily get discouraged by his weakness and clumsiness, especially if his first efforts for example to draw or to make something are discouraged, sometimes by well intentioned grown ups who try to help by doing something quickly and efficiently instead of letting him do it slowly and inefficiently. The growing child carries with him the memory of earlier failure and without much encouragement may acquire the habit of expecting to fail. He may put his hand to a succession of small projects such as collecting stamps, growing things in his own little patch of the garden, constructing do-it-yourself models or acquiring skill in some sport, only to find it difficult, to lose interest and to give up. The settled purpose to pursue some goal, however useless the goal from the point of view of the adult, and to forgo other interests and pleasures for the sake of it, is a big stride towards becoming responsible.

The last of the four strengths that a child needs to acquire if his growth to maturity is not to be held up is *competence*, which Erikson defines as 'the free exercise of dexterity and intelligence in the completion of tasks, unimpaired by infantile inferiority'. There are a number of skills important for a child's later life which can be acquired in childhood, usually without undue difficulty, with the right kind of encouragement. There are the social skills summed up in the phrase, good manners, the lack of which can prove a handicap later. There are the intellectual skills the foundations of which are laid in the three Rs. There are the manual skills, the learning to work with hands and do simple jobs efficiently.

These four virtues or strengths, hope, will, purpose and competence, are of importance all through life. They are especially important in childhood, not only because childhood is the time when they should be acquired, but also because their possession, at least to some modest degree, helps satisfactory growth through the storms of adolescence into the responsibility of adult life. They together contribute to what Erikson calls ego-strength, which roughly corresponds to what we mean by strength of character.

## THE GROWTH OF CONSCIENCE

One of the obstacles mentioned by Erikson that the child needs to surmount is an undue sense of guilt, which draws attention to the important subject of conscience. The first appearance of conscience, it would seem, occurs through the tendency of the small child to identify with parental attitudes and especially with parental approval of certain behaviour as good and with disapproval of other behaviour as bad. Thus the beginnings of conscience and a sense of duty appear to be socially determined. Whatever seed of conscience is implanted in us at birth it requires the influence of society to enable it to grow. A person believes he ought to be honest, truthful and considerate in the first place because others have told him that he ought. This socially instigated conscience is a rough and ready affair; its dictates are in general right but they lack flexibility and the power to discriminate. Also it can be far too strong and must be held responsible for destructively morbid guilt feelings. Indeed its voice sometimes resembles that of an inner policeman or hanging judge. There is another inner voice which addresses us with authority, the voice of our deepest insights. Though these insights have been educated by society and may often chime in with the voice of the socialised conscience, they sometimes clash with it. Sometimes I may have to disobey the voice of the socialised conscience, which corresponds to the opinions about right and wrong instilled by society, (or by that small unit of society which influences us most profoundly, our family) and to put up with the guilt feelings it may inflict, in order to be loyal to my deepest insights, my personal conscience. The origin of this personal conscience, it would seem, lies in the intimate personal relationship of a child with its mother. As a child I feel sorry for the first time, not because I have been blamed or reproved by anyone but because I have hurt someone I love. Loving relationship is the seed bed of this personal conscience and those who have never experienced this kind of relationship may never develop a personal conscience. Further the child's loving relationship with its mother is the root of a later conscious relationship with God.

The possession of two consciences, what I have called the personal conscience and the socialized conscience, can make moral decisions difficult, even agonising. It is bound up, I assume, with man's long period of immaturity. During that time of immaturity, which enables the human animal to assimilate much of the knowledge and experience of his elders, it is an advantage to him to be teachable, to give weight to what is told him by parents and teachers. No doubt part of what he learns is to develop his critical faculties, to use his own judgment and not to accept without question everything that he hears. But the precociously critical handicap themselves at a time when they should be gaining all they can from the wisdom of the tradition. As I see it both the personal conscience and the socialised conscience fall within God's guiding purpose for man. During the years of immaturity we are meant to be largely other-directed (that is guided by the wisdom of others) in order later to become inner-directed (that is guided by our own deepest wisdom). Certainly to become increasingly inner-directed seems to be the proper human aim to pursue 'You must call no-one on earth *father*, since you have only one Father and he is in heaven'.[11] No human figure is to be put in the place of God. Noone, neither my natural father nor some father figure, however rightly respected, can excuse me from facing the question, 'What do I in my heart of hearts think I ought to do?' For, in obeying our own deepest wisdom we are, to the best of our ability, obeying God. For this reason it has become a theological axiom that, despite the fallibility of conscience, conscience is to be obeyed.

To be inner directed, to be guided by one's own deepest wisdom approximates closely to the 'turning to the centre for guidance' of the last chapter. As I pointed out there the Christian can understand this living from the centre as being guided by God the God who has disclosed himself in Jesus Christ. He may make his own St Paul's 'I live, yet not I but Christ lives in me.'[12] Or he may understand the centre as that through which the transcendent God guides him and to see Christ as the icon of the Father, his way to the Father and the Father's word to him. But it is only when I have attained a certain maturity through having accomplished life's earlier tasks that it will be possible for me rightly to see my aim in the simple terms of living from the centre. A special task of childhood is the development of what Jung calls ego-consciousness and Erikson ego-strength. The integration of the personality cannot take place without the active cooperation of the conscious personality or ego, which Jung regards as the executive agent of the total personality the Self. From the point of view of the integration or individuation of the personality it is important in the first half of life that this executive agent should grow in consciousness and power and in the second half should learn to discover and submit to the deep centre.

Most of us who can look back at childhood from the vantage point of middle life are conscious of things that went wrong, of tasks never properly done, of lessons imperfectly learnt, which have hampered us as we faced later tasks and hamper us still. I believe that looking back with compassion and reliving the past, so far as memory permits, in the consciousness of God's active presence within us both then and now, is a valuable way of growing in self-awareness and in a creative relationship with the centre. Jesus said 'Except you become as little children you cannot enter the kingdom of God".[13] Looking back in the way I have indicated is one method of fostering the growth or recovery of a childlike spirit. Sometimes a person's painful and firmly repressed experiences in childhood cannot be recovered without the help of psychotherapy. The dialogue between patient and psychotherapist and the strong *rapport* established between them can enable the patient to recall, to speak about and finally to resolve the repressed emotions. All going well, the infantile fear, rage and despair, which, deeply buried in the soil of the unconscious, exercised a baleful influence on the patient's life, can be released and its harmful influence annulled.

The period of childhood is lived normally under the authority of parents and others such as school teachers, who share in a measure the parental role. If a child is to grow to maturity he must break out of the little parent dominated world and learn to stand on his own feet in the great world outside the home. This breaking free from the dependence of childhood and the beginning of real independence is one of the tasks of adolescence, which is the subject of our next chapter. But the better the tasks and lessons of childhood have been mastered the better equipped will be the boy or girl to embark on the next stage of the human journey.

1. Grove Press, New York, 1961.
2. André Deutsch. 1966.
3. Anthony Storr, *The Dynamics of Creation* (Secker & Warburg 1972) p. 123.
4. Op. cit. p. 125.

5. *The Inner Life of Man* (Methuen 1951) p. 251.
6. Quoted by G.R. Taylor in *Rethink* (Penguin 1975) pp. 123–4.
7. *Cycles of Affirmation* (Darton, Longman and Todd 1975) p. 11.
8. Op. cit. p. 19.
9. Op. cit. p. 92.
10. See *Insight and Responsibility* (Norton 1962) pp. 113–124.
11. Matthew. 23.9.
12. Galatians 2.20.
13. Matthew 18. 3.

# 4. Age of Uncertainty

April is the cruelest month
Breeding lilacs out of the dead land
Stirring dull roots with spring rain.

                              T.S. Eliot, *Waste Land* ll. 1–3

The opening lines of Eliot's *Waste Land* contradict the superficial popular notion that happiness is typical of youth. No doubt youth and more particularly adolescence has a capacity for rapturous joy; but much more typical of it are moods of uncertainty, self-doubt and depression. Much has been written about adolescence. The point of view of this chapter is twofold. First it seeks to show this stage of life in the context of God's presence within it and his purpose for the whole of life. Second it aims to help people in middle life to understand their own adolescence better, to recall its crises and to face its unresolved problems, in order to possess themselves more completely and attain a greater selfawareness.

## THE CRISES OF ADOLESCENCE

The urge to self-realization, one of the basic assumptions of psychotherapy, is awakened and fostered both by pressures from within the personality and from circumstances outside it. As was pointed out in the last chapter, the task of the first half of life is the building up of a strong ego, which I see as consisting at the end of childhood in Erikson's four strengths of childhood hope, will, purpose and competence. The development of this strong conscious personality proceeds by way of successive crises which are essentially growing pains. The crisis is caused by the conflict between the habits and attitude built up as an adaptation to an earlier stage of life and the pressure both of inner urges and needs and changed outer circumstances which make the old attitude inappropriate and ineffective. The conflict can only be resolved by modifying the old attitude in order to adjust to the new pressures. For example a child going for the first time to the infant school is plunged into a crisis as he finds that the tears or bursts of rage with which he was accustomed to get his way in the home are no longer appropriate or effective. He has to learn from the example of other children, the help of his teacher, and the support of his home, to grow up a little, to make a better adaptation to the demands of school. The slow growth of the conscious personality can be likened to a young king learning with the help of tutors and guardians to assume rule over his kingdom. The urges, drives and impulses which the young personality can only with difficulty control are like rebellious elements in the kingdom which may be kept under for a time by police or the military. Some kind of law and order is established and there follows a temporary peace. But sooner or later a stronger rebellion breaks out, which can only be dealt with satisfactorily by admitting the legitimacy of some of its grievances and allowing to its representatives a place in the government. In some such way the consciousness is enlarged and extended. This is a process that continues through life, periods of relative peace being succeeded by crisis and conflict which lead to further growth in consciousness and a more stable peace. These successive crises can be understood as crises of death and rebirth, the death of an old attitude to life and the birth of a new, which turns out in fact to be the old attitude renewed.

This process of growth through facing and surmounting crises is enormously intensified in adolescence. The crisis is triggered off by the onset of puberty at an age which varies from 11 to 15. There is a sudden spurt of growth, an accession of increased strength and energy together with the activation

of the glands which control sexual development. The relatively
stable world of childhood is shattered by these new, exciting
and not yet manageable powers, emotions and impulses. The
sudden spurt of sexual development with its accompanying
bodily changes commonly awakens curiosity and the desire to
experiment by some kind of sex play, perhaps by mastur-
bation, perhaps by actual sexual intercourse. In some cases
this leaves a legacy of guilt feeling. At this time the boy or girl
feels embarrassed and ashamed in situations in which he
would have been at home a year or two before. The inner tur-
moil of adolescence has been compared with that of infancy
with its helplessness, its frustrations and humiliations. The
infant finds himself thrust into a strange world which he faces
with mingled fear and curiosity. Similarly the adolescent after
the comparative calm and stability of childhood is plunged
into a new world that is both thrilling and frightening. The
newness is caused by the burgeoning of powerful energies
within himself chief of which is sex. In the wake of these inner
forces are drawn the imperfectly solved problems and crises of
infancy, which had been kept under during childhood, but
now break out all over again. For example a boy when a small
child was over-dependent on the reassurance of his mother or
father. In the fairly protected world of later childhood, he has
apparently grown out of this childish clinging to authority,
only to find that the inner upheaval and uncertainty of
adolescence has brought back a feeling of insecurity and the
need of some authoritative person to reassure him. Again there
may come a recrudescence of the humiliation, the sense of
being useless and ridiculous that reduced him to tears when he
was little. His initiative is undermined, he dithers and cannot
make up his mind. Or again he may be possessed by a
moodiness, an inability to settle to anything or to complete a
task that he has undertaken. He may become less capable and
reliable than he was a year or two before. He may become
oafish, clumsy and lose all confidence in his intelligence and
practical capacity.

These and other characteristics of adolescence can be understood as regression, a return to a childish attitude imperfectly grown out of; it looks like a relapse. But it is also an
instinctive method of facing and dealing with an unresolved

conflict from the past. It is as though a badly set limb has to be broken again before it can be reset. The process is wholly unconscious and indeliberate. Somehow the loosening or even the complete break up of the attitude of late childhood allows into the daylight of consciousness the dark, unsatisfied longings, the feelings of rage and resentment, of helpless dependence, of depression and despair that lie buried deep within. The adolescent becomes aware of these dark forces mainly indirectly through the phenomenon called projection. A boy with a deeply repressed need for protection may find himself compulsively attracted by some fatherly or motherly figure, possibly a school teacher or scoutmaster. Such a figure acts as a powerful focus for the boy's deep down longing; much childish feeling becomes constellated in and directed upon this figure of authority. A girl who as an infant felt herself to be unloved and thought inferior to her baby brother may get it into her head that everyone despises her and thinks her plain and unattractive. She is projecting her own feeling of being despised or disregarded onto other people whose real opinions may be totally different. Unfortunately, by acting as though others find us dull and unattractive we may force our view of ourselves on to them so that they accept it as true.

Projection, the reading into others of qualities that are really in ourselves, takes place everywhere, especially where people are living or working at close quarters, as in home or school. It is by no means merely a mistake and can assist the growth of the personality, particularly when a person begins to realise and relinquish his projections. I may learn in time to recognise unknown facts about myself as I see them reflected in the mirror of another's personality. At first I am wholly unaware of what is happening. What I am conscious of is an unaccountable, a quasi-magical attraction to the other person. The fascination is due to the fact that he activates something deep in myself, his words carry a resonance that echoes and reechoes within. In time the spell of his personality wears off, I rub my eyes and perceive that he is just an ordinary person. I had been reading something of myself into him. And with the withdrawal of the projection I find that I have gained possession of part of myself of which I had been unconscious.

My consciousness has been enlarged; I feel myself a stronger, more complete person.

The psychic mechanism of projection helps to account for hero worship and falling in love both of them characteristic of adolescence. A boy or girl often makes a hero of someone of the same sex but a year or two older. Under the idolatry of his hero he is apt to take over more or less uncriticised the ideas and aims of his idol and, in order to conform to them, will begin to change his style of dress and behaviour and discipline himself by giving up childish pleasures. The phase of hero worship does not as a rule last long, but while it lasts it is a potent influence in the life of a boy or girl. Adolescence is a time when boys and girls tend to form intense, affectionate attachments, at first with a member of their own sex and later with one of the opposite.

Through friendship the boy or girl is drawn into the unfamiliar world of another personality with a different background and different interests. He begins to discover himself, his own bent, his own aptitudes and ineptitudes by contrast with another whom friendship has made intimate and familiar. Friendships in adolescence are as a rule neither deep nor lasting. It is a time of exploration and experiment particularly in the sphere of relationships in which boys and girls try out different roles with a succession of friends. By partial identification with first one friend and then another they not only develop different elements of their personality but also they come to see which of them matters most to them and begin to realise what sort of persons they are. Only when a person is coming to be clear about what he wants from life is he able to commit himself wholeheartedly to another. As a rule this will not be until the end of adolescence, and this firmer grasp of his identity may well mark the division between adolescence and adulthood.

Not only is there a tendency during adolescence to make heroes, that is to see others as the larger than life embodiment of longings and aspirations in ourselves. There is a similar tendency to create villains, oppressors, who activate deep within us painful and humiliating experiences which are partly or totally forgotten. Just as one person makes me feel relaxed and happy, so another perhaps by his mere presence brings out the worst in me. Very often parents are the recipients of these negative projections. It may be that feelings of guilt rooted deeply in past experience and strongly repressed are aroused by a particular schoolmaster or maybe by my own father. And if my father has occasion to criticise me an immense surge of resentment mounts up out of all proportion to his mild and reasonable remonstrances. There are special reasons why adolescents are often ill at ease with their parents. For the teenage boy or girl has to grow out of the dependence of an obedient child into the self-reliance of one who must choose his own path and make his own decisions. The period of transition from childhood to adulthood requires a gradual relinquishment of authority by the parents and a corresponding growth of autonomy in the sons and daughters. The tensions of this transition time are liable to be complicated by a blindness in both parents and their offspring. The latter are usually very conscious of a desire for the maximum possible freedom and independence but are blind to a deep-seated tendency to cling to and rely on persons who for most of their lives have been their major source of security. The parents on the other hand are commonly outspoken in expressing their hope that their young will grow up and learn to behave responsibly, while deep down they hanker for the days when their children were wholly dependent on them, a hankering that is liable to undermine their purpose to help them to become independent. The tensions between parents and their teenage sons and daughters are liable to be greater and more prolonged for the minority who are at school or college during the whole of adolescence. It is difficult to be free of the authority of parents when one is economically dependent on them. It is difficult for parents to concede complete freedom to those whom they are supporting and subsidising financially.

The partly inevitable conflicts of outlook between teenage boys and girls and their parents throws them upon the society of their peers. This is made easy by the fact that school brings them into touch with many whom they would not have met at home. For some school is a kind of prison, a necessary evil perhaps, but an experience to be got through as quickly and painlessly as possible. But for many it is a time of mental and spiritual awakening. The natural curiosity of some is caught and held and fostered by science or history and may grow into a passion to know. The aesthetic sensibility of others is awakened by poetry, literature, art, or music. Some are set on fire by a social passion to make the world a better place, which may feed an interest in politics or the social sciences. The exploration of new regions of knowledge and beauty opened up by older teachers is at its best a shared voyage of discovery with friends of one's own age fostered by argument and the sharing of experience. But side by side with this growing assimilation of the tradition of culture and civilisation there is also a growth in self-understanding, the beginning of an individual point of view based not on the authority of others but, at least in part, on thought out belief and personal vision. The strength of this growing sense of personal identity is measured by nothing so well as by the anger and violence with which a boy or girl reacts to any attempt by parents or any one else to impose a role or career upon him which clashes with what he feels himself to be. This resistance to the impositions of authority is strengthened by teenage solidarity. For the local group or gang based on school or neighbourhood gives moral support to its members, and will occasionally impose its opinions, its standards of behaviour and style of dress with an authority which no parent would venture to assert. But beyond the local group and influencing it is the fairly new phenomenon of a youth culture, spread by T.V., radio and record, with its pop music and youthful stars, which influences teenagers of every social stratum and background. This youth culture has helped to widen the 'generation gap' and accentuated the age old division between the young and their elders.

Under the varied influences of home and school and neighbourhood, of peer groups and youth culture, the adolescent steers his way across the gulf which separates childhood from adulthood. Erikson gives to the strength needed for the voyage of adolescence the name fidelity, which he defines as 'the ability to sustain loyalties freely pledged in spite of the inevitable contradictions of value systems'. The teenage schoolboy needs a certain courage if he is to be loyal to his intimate friends, to the larger, perhaps somewhat philistine, group to which he is attached and to his parents and family.

The three loyalties may pull him in different directions. One boy will be tempted to avoid the strain by trying to be all things to all men, to take on chameleon-like the colour of his company; to be a philistine with the philistines and a lover of poetry with the literati, to be the obedient son at home and the merciless critic of his parents with his friends. He escapes tension at the price of knowing himself to be something of a traitor. Another evasion of the tension is to try to opt out of one or other of the loyalties. A tough and insensitive boy may be cold and non-cooperative at home and spend as much of his time as possible out with his friends. The sensitive, intellectual boy may try to run as a lone wolf and refuse to associate more than he can help with the perhaps rowdy group to which he is linked. Fidelity includes not only loyalty to persons but to principles and values, to the good, the true and the beautiful. During this period the teenage boy or girl, both consciously and unconsciously, is searching for a personality image both true to his character and acceptable to others, which will enable him to take his place unashamed in the adult world.


## THE PERSONALITY IDEAL

Both the personality image and the personality ideal play an important part in the growth of the personality. I referred earlier to the inborn urge to self-realization which prompts and pricks the individual to explore and experiment, especially in the field of relationships, and so gradually to discover his aptitudes and develop his talents. One expression of this urge is the formation of a personality ideal the roots of which are in childhood. To begin with the small child models himself, partly by unconscious imitation, partly deliberately, on his parents; the boy normally wants to be like father, the girl like mother. Later, loved and respected relatives, teachers or friends modify the ideal. Nationality and social background affect the personality ideal. The english idea of what a man or woman should be differs slightly from that of the scottish, the french and the american. The son of a stevedore is likely to have a different personality ideal from the son of a doctor. But however much these ideals are influenced or even taken over secondhand from parents or school friends they will be in part individual. Very commonly there springs up a conflict between a boy's or girl's personal ideal, not necessarily explicitly formulated, and his parent's aims for him, and this conflict tends to come to a head during adolescence.

Looked at within the context of a person's whole life story a personality ideal which accords reasonably well with his gifts and aptitudes is a great help to developing the ego strength, the strength of character, which enables him to carry out responsibly the tasks of adult life. But a personality ideal can never completely accord with a person's true potential and it can easily be used in all innocence as a means of rejecting apparently undesirable elements of the personality and of evading challenges which ought to be faced. The subject is important enough to deserve to be illustrated at length, and to do this I will sketch in barest outline four imaginary characters.

Samuel was a sensitive and somewhat timid child. Once when he was small he was badly frightened by a large dog which jumped up at him and knocked him down. On another occasion he was bullied and ridiculed by some older children. He never spoke to anyone about these and many similar experiences. He wanted to forget about them and succeeded in doing so to a large extent by turning to fantasy. He imagined himself in a castle so strongly fortified that no enemy could force his way in and he himself was quite safe. At school he never fought and he took care to avoid any dispute that might lead to blows. He greatly admired his father, a man of gentle and placid disposition, and as he grew older he consciously formed the aim of facing life like his father with quiet confidence. Samuel's calm and gentle manner attracted a number of boys who sought his friendship, but those who knew him well were not quite happy about his calmness which did not always ring true. He had a reluctance to face disagreeable facts. He was fond of saying when others expressed alarm 'Don't worry, everything will be all right'. Sometimes this did indeed happen. But when it didn't, when a crisis blew up which faced earlier could have been averted he was apt to go to pieces, his facade of calm disintegrated and he became anxious and frightened and unable to cope. Plainly there was something wrong with Samuel's manner of facing difficulty.

His ideal, useful up to a point and in some situations, was inadequate. It had been adopted partly, like the fantasy of the impregnable castle, to enable him to escape from the painful feeling of fear which had been his bugbear in early childhood and had haunted him ever since. For in fact the capacity to be afraid is necessary for survival in an unsafe world. Sensitivity to danger, if it does not overwhelm us, alerts all our faculties to counter the danger.

My second illustration is Nancy, a very different child from Samuel. As a baby she used to erupt like a volcano if she was not given what she wanted on the instant. It sometimes looked as though she was possessed by a murderous hate against those who kept her waiting. Her mother came in for a lot of this and she used to become quite alarmed by her demon daughter. After a little while Nancy began to sense her mother's alarm and began to be afraid too. She feared that her mother hated her tantrums and did not love her when she behaved like that. So it became important to her not only to get over her rages in order to please her mother but in general to win her love by being a good girl. The lesson was reinforced when she went to school and learnt that losing her temper not only made her unpopular but the object of ridicule. She was an affectionate girl and could not bear to be cold shouldered. So gradually she formed the aim of getting everyone's approval by being nice to them. She threw herself into the activities of the youth group to which she belonged, was always ready to shoulder more than her share of any chores and became very popular. But for all that everyone liked her people who knew her well could not fail to notice a weakness in her. She was too anxious to please and would be quite cast down if her kind and unselfish actions were not noticed. Her close friends sometimes found it a little wearing to have to administer pats on the back to cheer her up. The desire to please is a normal characteristic and a person wholly devoid of it would be impossible to live with. But in Nancy's case it had assumed an altogether exaggerated place in her system of values, because it was her defence against the threat of being rejected. In order not to give offence she had been driven to suppress a great deal of herself, in particular her natural forcefulness. For though unrestrained anger can be very destructive there is a fighting spirit proper to man, which under control supplies the driving power within the virtues of fortitude, perseverance and patience.

My third example I will call Peter. As a small boy he was puny and delicate, his elder brother used to tease him for being so small and his father used to say in a mock serious voice 'You'll never do any good'. Little Peter hated this and felt intensely humiliated by the teasing. He said little but he determined that one day he would prove that he was somebody and compel his father and brother to recognise the fact. At school he was not good at games but he was of above average intelligence and his ambition drove him to work hard. He was not popular with other boys, and his caustic tongue and his obstinacy in pursuing an argument to the bitter end made him a little feared. But he did well in his A levels and had no difficulty in getting a place in a university where he did well academically.    At the university he became a keen christian to the surprise of his friends, for he was unmistakably ambitious. When challenged about this he said that he was ambitious for the Kingdom. But the old Adam was by no means dead in him. Sometimes he would give you the impression that he was over-conscious of being a prominent christian. If you argued or disagreed with him he was apt to make some snubbing remark that left you feeling sore. He was only really happy with those who looked up to him as a leader, and to them he could be a powerful friend. He was prominent in protesting against racial discrimination and always ready to lend his support to any down-trodden minority. On the other hand he was not at all sympathetic towards the weak and the unsuccessful when he actually met them as individuals. In his heart he despised weakness. He hated anything that reminded him of the painful feeling of weakness that had been cruelly rubbed into him when he was little. So, though he crusaded on behalf of the weak, partly because his religion impelled him to, partly because he secretly loved a fight, he never really liked them nor they him. He had turned an ambition to succeed into an idol, because it seemed the surest way of banishing from his mind the painful humiliations of his childhood. Clearly to aim at being a success is wholly legitimate. It would be a poor look out if we did not hope to make a success of what we undertake.

But to attach absolute importance to personal success as Peter did means inevitably the stunting of our humanity.

My final illustration shall be Rachel, who as a baby somewhat resembled Nancy. Frequent squalls of rage used to shake her like Nancy at the inevitable frustrations of infant life. But she reacted to her mother's disapproval of her tantrums in a quite different way from the other girl. Rachel so identified with her mother's disapproval that she came to feel that she was thoroughly bad. She began to fear and hate the rages that like an evil demon used to take possession of her and estrange her from her mother. This painful feeling of being bad deep down which began in infancy played a large part in her development. She felt urged at all costs to escape from it. The road she took was that of trying hard to be good, not like Nancy in order to please her mother, only a minor consideration with Rachel, but in order to banish from her mind the painful feeling of guilt. Her mother who was a religious woman understood very little of what was going on in her Rachel, who was becoming a prig. But we cannot ascribe Rachel's development entirely to her mother's treatment of her, for her younger sister who underwent the same treatment was a naughty little monkey who reacted to her elder sister's conscientiousness with a cheerful disregard of the rules of the home. Rachel early discovered that her good behaviour earned her certain advantages over her feckless younger sister, but she noticed too with chagrin that her sister was her mother's favourite. Rachel grew up a conscientious girl in a somewhat negative manner. She could be relied upon to keep out of mischief and to refrain from generally recognized wrong doing, but she showed little initiative in doing right. As she grew older she developed a holier-than-thou attitude, especially towards the girls of her acquaintance, which naturally did not endear her to them, and she was deeply shocked at some of their affairs. In fact she was inclined to be critical of most people and to move in an atmosphere of moral superiority. Clearly, Rachel's ideal of good behaviour was inadequate. Motive is all important for the assessment of good actions and her motive was neither love of goodness nor love of people but the desire to think well of herself and banish the feeling of guilt with which she had been saddled in childhood.

The four character sketches that I have outlined bring out clearly the inadequacy of the personality ideal in each case. But none of the ideals was ignoble even though each left something to be desired. Samuel's ideal was that of quiet confidence, Nancy's was to give pleasure to others, Peter's to be a success in a good cause, Rachel's to live a good life. Each of the ideals was too narrowly conceived and in each case the motive was defective. But the possession of an ideal helped to give to them all a certain strength of character, a purpose that enabled them to steer their way through the rocks and shoals that can shipwreck the adolescent. Further the ideals were developed as an attempt to cope with crises whose origins were in infancy or early childhood, crises for which they were in no way to blame.

The attempts were not wholly successful. They did not resolve the crises, but rather incorporated them into the ideal in such a way as to contribute, not altogether happily, to their way of facing the demands of growing up, and preparing for adult responsibility. Each of them will have to face his unresolved crisis later if he is to grow to his full human stature. In the next chapter I shall suggest ways in which this may come about.

## THE RELIGION OF ADOLESCENTS

But I cannot end this chapter without referring to the religion of adolescents. Many people reckon the years between the age of thirteen and nineteen as the time when religion began to become an important, perhaps the most important, fact in their lives. I believe that God, present to each and every man makes use of many means, singly or in combination, to rouse people from their unawareness. Perhaps the most important of these means is the affirmation of religious truth with conviction. Faith is caught not taught; fire kindles fire. Sometimes the fire is kindled through formal preaching at a church service, sometimes through the sharing of conviction in an informal group, sometimes through one to one witness in private conversation. The apparent irrationality of what is sometimes preached is not necessarily a barrier to it being received, for genuine conviction is attractive in itself to those who are uncertain, and we may accept without question that a preacher is speaking of realities he knows at first hand, even while we discount some of his reasoning and explanation. This tendency to bypass reasoning in order to grasp spiritual reality intuitively may partly explain the attraction of the young to fundamentalism whether of an infallible Bible or an infallible Church. Both Bible and Church are powerful symbols pointing to the reality of the living God, and the intellectual difficulties of believing either to be inerrant may be felt to be insignificant by comparison with the spiritual power of the symbol. Another factor predisposing a person to the gospel is a sense of moral bankruptcy, which the adolescent sometimes feels acutely; the sense of failure at not living up to one's ideal, the gap between the personality ideal (what I aim at) and the personality image (what I see myself to be). A gospel that promises both inner healing and moral power speaks straight to the condition of the morally defeated.

Sometimes God discloses himself through beauty which St Augustine called the splendour of truth. Music and art and above all nature have power to expand our everyday awareness so as to grasp realities that eye has not seen nor ear heard. The gorgeous sunset, the majestic mountain range, the wide-stretching view can speak powerfully of God's presence. It was the sight of a tree stripped of its leaves in the winter that brought home the reality of God's presence to the eighteen year old Nicholas Herman, better known as Brother Lawrence, the name he adopted when he became a Carmelite friar, and for his spiritual classic, *The Practice of the Presence of God*. Those who already possess the conceptual framework of Christian belief can more readily recognize in nature's mysterious power over the human spirit the presence of God. Without the framework of belief in God a person might not know how to interpret the experience. Sometimes a disclosure of the reality of God is granted after a period of wrestling, like Job, with the problems of existence. Why does anything exist? What could have set the evolutionary process going? Why is there so much apparent evil and injustice? The answer comes not from logic but through a certainty of God that floods into consciousness creating an assurance of the truth of religion. The fact that this awareness of God is often focused in some object or scene outside us does not contradict the directions of the old spiritual guides who tell us to look for God within. For it is an inner voice or an inner feeling that enables us to perceive God in the external world.

There appears to be a turning away from institutional religion among the young today. Two factors contribute to this revulsion. The first is that it is impossible in a time of rapid social change like the present for a venerable institution like the Church to keep pace with the changes. In consequence like other old institutions it tends to look incongruous and out of date in its modern setting. The second is that many young people are thoroughly disillusioned by the materialist goals of modern western civilization and look upon the Church as part of an establishment that they would like to see radically altered if not destroyed. But the figure of Jesus as portrayed in the gospels still strongly attracts the young. His courage and integrity and compassion are qualities they admire and would like to possess. In their uncertainty and vulnerability they can easily identify with one who challenged the powers that be and made no attempt to protect himself from their hostility. In the heart of the young christian who believes that Jesus is alive and invites men to place themselves under his leadership, the words 'Follow me' echo and reecho with a persuasiveness that he cannot easily forget.

In the previous chapter I spoke of the value of looking back with compassion on our childhood, whose painful memories live on within us. The same applies to the years of uncertainty, when perhaps for the first time the reality of God and the power of religion dawned on us, when with many moments of embarrassment and self-consciousness, of excitement and happiness, of depression and resentment we grew from children into men and women. These years are nearer to us than the years of childhood and more easily remembered. But though we may envy the animal spirits, the sensual gusto and the bouncing resilience of our teens, we may find it hard to forgive the brutalities, the crude experiments with sex, the wasted opportunities, the unfulfilled promise. All the same the impress of our adolescence remains within us and contributes to making us what we are; and to be able to recall, without either condoning or repudiating, the actions and experiences of those past years is one of the roads to self-awareness in the present.

# 5. The Years of Responsibility

Not the intense moment
Isolated, with no before and after,
But a lifetime burning in every moment
                                    T.S. Eliot, *East Coker* ll.192-4

If Christianity is true, man's destiny lies beyond this world, which must be seen in one aspect as a vale of soul-making. But it contradicts belief in God as Creator to understand the world as it has sometimes been understood as nothing but a vale of soul-making. The God who clothes the lily and cares for each sparrow must be concerned for the well-being and fulfilment of man in this life. These superficially opposed points of view are reconciled if we see the fulfilment of man's earthly tasks as one of the ways in which the 'inexhaustible power for good and the inexhaustible fund of invention and contrivance' persuades man to prepare for union with himself and fosters the life that grows and expands beyond the confines of this world. The years of childhood and adolescence are both a preparation for the tasks of adulthood and a laying of the foundations of a relationship to God which is to last into eternity.

## THE TASKS OF ADULTHOOD

There is no biological change to mark the transition from adolescence to adulthood such as marks the transition from childhood to adolescence. For this reason it is impossible to say at what age persons become adult. One man may seem grown up at eighteen while another seems utterly irresponsible at twenty-one. There is a gradual assumption of responsibility by an individual in late adolescence and a slow recognition by society of the fact. Certain landmarks indicate the attainment of adult status: marriage, establishment in a job or career and financial independence. Strong social pressure supports the natural concern of the individual to become independent. He is heir to a culture and civilization built by the labours of countless men and women most of them dead. He has been supported by the care and work of parents, school teachers and many others of the generation immediately preceding his own. What we have received constitutes a debt which we can only discharge by working and caring for the generations following. What we have received from the past is repaid to the future. Perhaps the transition to adulthood might be described as the change from being predominantly a receiver into becoming increasingly a giver. This increasing responsibility and care for others is not just a duty, it is the only road to fulfilment. It is also a necessary part of a genuine relationship to God.

If we realise ourselves as we learn to care for and give to others, only the love and intimate friendship of others awakens this capacity for altruism. There are different levels and kinds of intimacy. There is the need for bodily closeness which is at its height in infancy, grows less with increasing years, but never wholly disappears. This is partly satisfied in the physical intimacy of the sexual act. The ecstatic element in sexual intercourse helps to knit two disparate human beings into union on a deep, basic earthy level. But at the same time the bodily intimacy of the sexual act awakens infantile emotions of greed, possessiveness and jealousy which can disturb and threaten the relationship. The personal intimacy of friendship in which two people share ideas, feelings and aims sometimes leads to marriage and may be strengthened by the close proximities of the wedded state. But it is by no means confined to marriage or to any other relationship in which physical sex predominates; and as everyone knows it can be entirely lacking between marriage partners. Further some of those who choose to remain

celibate find that their freedom from the ties of marriage with
its ecstasies and its frustrations enables them to form close
friendships at a deeper level and with a wider circle than.
would have been possible had they married. Sex is a fundamental part of the humanity of all men and women. Freud
distinguishes between affective and genital or reproductive
sexuality. These two elements though closely linked are distinct and, though the genital is essential for the maintenance of
the race, the affective element is more important for friendship
and enters into all warm and intimate relationships, including
many which would not generally be thought of as sexual. We
need close friendship if we are to live our lives to the full. To
quote words of Dr Dominian: 'We need others to help us to see
ourselves, to reach those bits of ourselves that are unconscious
or have never developed. Having been assisted in this way, we
still need them for a period in an exchange in which we learn
new ways of feeling and reacting. It is not enough to understand intellectually the nature of the problem, we have to
learn step by step new patterns of emotional behaviour; and
for this we need the help, encouragement and support of
others who love us as they need us to love them.' [1]

At the same time, though we need intimacy we also fear it,
for it can be a threat to our integrity, our deepest beliefs and
highest values. For intimacy means exposing myself, what I
really am, to the scrutiny of another. I fear blame or ridicule or
being dominated by or becoming over-dependent on someone
else. The closer I am to another the more liable I am to receive
or give unintended hurt. Part of me would be glad to expose
myself if only I could be sure that the other person would not
take advantage of my admissions. But another part of me is
afraid. So I am inclined to hold back, to be on the defensive. I
will allow a little intimacy but too much would be dangerous.

What impels the majority of people to lower their defences
and to open themselves to another is the immensely powerful
drive of sex. Two people in love are propelled into intimacy by
their mutual attachment. It is easy to sentimentalise over
lovers and to gloze over the pain, the personal damage they
sometimes suffer through mistakes encouraged by a false
romanticism. If we rightly understand man as being on the
move, as being pressed by the Creator to develop his human

potential and grow towards the fully human man of the future, then one of the urgent tasks of the human race is to humanize the powerful sex drive. This drive inherited from our animal ancestors and essential for the propagation of our species, needs to be humanized by bringing it under the sway of a caring love that seeks personal intimacy more than physical delight and the good of the other for his or her own sake. Marriage, in all its varied forms, is the institution built up to safeguard humanity, to prevent socially destructive sex rivalry and to protect the needs of children. The successful marriage depends in the long run less on physical attraction than on personal affection, on the mutual desire to explore with respect and sensitivity the mystery of the other's personality, and on the will to cooperate in the building of a home and the bringing up of children. The love that makes possible a good marriage includes the willingness to lose oneself, to take the risk of being let down, to give oneself.

One simple way to a clearer understanding of the complex mystery of love is to see in it two distinct elements. There is first the delight in the other which can be of many kinds from physical ecstasy to aesthetic pleasure, from the enjoyment of the company of the other to the comfort and security of having someone who will do things for one. But in addition to the element of pleasure we have in someone we love, there is a caring quality, a love of the person for himself or herself, a desire even a determination to put the good of the other before one's own interest. These two elements in loving, the caring element and the element of delight support and complement each other, but the caring element is the more essential and, where the element of delight outweighs the caring, love is to that extent spoilt. Many people when they enter on marriage are incapable, owing to a legacy of unsolved problems from the past, of giving themselves in unselfish appreciation of and devotion to another. A common cause of marital breakdown is some unsatisfied emotional need dating from early childhood. Such an unsatisfied need may lead a person to seek through marriage the solution of a problem that would  have been solved years before had early upbringing been more fortunate. The immature child buried within a man may press him into trying to turn his wife into a mother who will take care of him and coddle him. The wife equally may be pressed by some childish need never adequately satisfied into making impossible demands on her husband. No doubt all people approach marriage hampered by unsatisfied emotional needs from the past and if these needs are not excessive marriage may prove their solution. To be loved by another triggers off my capacity to love unselfishly and the mutual love of the partners in a good marriage can strengthen the caring love of both. This caring love will be both expressed and deepened through the shared task of bringing up children.

Society's expectation that young men and women should get married, helpful in forcing them to face this issue is harmful if it leads them into marriage before they are mature enough to build a stable marriage relationship. Another expectation of society that presses upon the young adult is that he should support himself by work. Work helps a person to gain the self-assurance that comes from the recognition of his worth by his fellows. The unemployed have their self-respect undermined, they tend to feel that society has no use for them, painful childhood memories of feeling themselves to be no good are reactivated. Work helps a man to realise himself especially when the work is of a kind to call out his talents and enable him to express himself in it, and devote himself to it. For many the choice of what job they go to is minimal. They are forced to take what work is available. All the same, though at the outset there may have been small choice, there is sometimes the opportunity later of turning to the kind of work that can be seen as a vocation, if a person is prepared to make a financial sacrifice.

Again a job or career which in some way involves the care for or service of people will satisfy a deep human need, the need to be needed. No doubt for many people this need is amply satisfied in the bringing up of a family. But the need to care for people and serve them is the mainspring in the life of a large number of people, from nurses and teachers to probation officers and welfare workers and to the large number of persons who undertake voluntary social work in their spare-time. A number of motives may lead a person to take up politics, whether local or national, among them the desire for power and influence and public recognition. But a major motive is the

desire to be of service to other people and to work for the
common good.


## STAGES IN ADULT LIFE

There are stages in adult life. In early adulthood a person
needs to establish himself in financial independence, probably
to marry and build a stable relationship with the marriage
partner and share in the task of building a home. Then he will
be concerned to make a success of his job or career. These
tasks coming all together are likely to absorb most of his
energies for ten years or more. The time will come, perhaps in
his thirties, when he is sufficiently established or at least
knows where he stands in these first tasks. He will feel a need
to take up interests that he had been forced to forgo, to come
to terms with rejected bits of his own personality and to look
again at unfaced personal problems. There should come a
broadening and deepening of his outlook. One of the concerns
that a person often suppresses in his effort to establish himself
is religion. And where this has happened it is likely to return
with questionings about what life is for and what he ought to
do with his life.

A broadening of interests and a fuller self-acceptance fits a
person better both for the greater responsibilities he is likely to
have to carry in his prime and also for the deepening of a
relationship with God. If all goes well a person is likely to grow
in genuine altruism, an altruism that is both spontaneous and
enriching. He will tend increasingly to enjoy doing things for
people and will be ready to volunteer for the jobs, in home or
church or neighbourhood or the larger world, that need doing.
With the approach of old age, all being well, a person tends to
mellow, to grow more tolerant, to become wiser. He readily
gives up responsibility to others, relinquishes action for contemplation; he looks back with gratitude and forward with
confidence and hope as he faces death and the unknown that
lies beyond death.

In this brief glance at the responsibilities of adult life I have
felt obliged to ignore the large question mark set against

western civilisation, with its goal of an ever rising standard of living, which appears to be heading towards one or more of several different kinds of world catastrophe. There have always been a few who have opted out of some of the responsibilities of society in order to affirm the absolute primacy of God. Many more today are finding themselves impelled to witness to the truth that man does not live by bread alone by the deliberate choice of a life of simplicity. There are others who work and struggle to bring about a reconstruction of society on juster and more human lines. But to examine these movements of protest would take us right outside the limited aims of this book.

I have spoken of a person's likely development if things go well with him; but sometimes things go badly. The demands of adult life press us to go forward whether or not we are ready to advance. Noone enters upon adulthood with the tasks of his early life perfectly completed and its lessons thoroughly learnt. The most that anyone achieves is to get through adequately. This does not mean that we are necessarily much to blame. The worst handicaps are those whose origin is in infancy and childhood, for which we cannot fairly be blamed. Those who are free from serious handicap are the fortunate. Only as we attain a certain 'ego strength' do we become capable of actions deserving either of much credit or of much blame. But it is an important task for personal growth to come to terms with the failures, the evasions and the wasted opportunities of the past.

We can see a little of what this might involve by returning to the four characters of the last chapter. Each of them had in growing up adopted a personality ideal which, though perhaps the best he was capable of when it was formed, involved running away from an experience too painful to face. Each of them if he is to grow to his full human stature, must face and learn to accept part of himself that he is rejecting. Samuel must learn that a tranquil mind is excellent where it can be maintained but must not be made an excuse for evading difficult people or unpleasant situations. If he is to grow he must be ready to face aggressive men or women, determined to have their way, a thing that Peter would not think twice about. Samuel however hates such confrontations and has to learn to face difficulty even though his knees are knocking together.

He must learn to live with anxiety without either running away from worrying facts or burying his head in the sand and ignoring their existence. If he will do this he will find that anxiety becomes manageable and he will grow as a person. If he fails to do this his deep down timidity will become more pronounced. More and more of his energy will be taken up with avoiding trouble. As a person he will narrow and diminish and very likely in the end he will fail to avoid the trouble he fears.

Nancy if she is to continue to grow as a person must stop being so anxious to please. Her ideal of serving other people and being nice to them is excellent, but to serve a person's real interests is not necessarily to fall in with his wishes. Sometimes when a person is fishing for flattery it is kindest to state the unpalatable truth. Faithful are the wounds of a friend. Nancy must learn to face her deep fear of unpopularity, of being rejected, and learn to say what she really feels and refuse to say only what will please. She will have to battle with the habit of years  to say smooth things. This will go deeply against the grain and she may have to be forced into breaking the habit. Some action of hers to her great surprise awakens bitter opposition. All her instincts prompt her to backpedal, to run for cover, to give in to the opposition. But though this might sometimes be the right course she knows that in this instance it would be wrong. Not only is her project at stake but her own soul's health and freedom. Only when she has learnt to face opposition and unpopularity will she be able genuinely to fulfil her ideal of service. Unless she can learn to face her fear of rejection she is likely to grow increasingly disappointed and cynical.

Peter, superficially at least, the most outstanding of our imaginary quartet, has a great deal to learn if he is to do the great things for the Kingdom that he professes to aim at. People who know him well prophesy a successful career whether in the service of the State, the Church or some humanitarian cause. But if he is to develop his human capacity to the full he must stop making an idol of success. He likes to be in a position of authority and he enjoys directing the actions and lives of others. But if he is to grow as a person he must be willing to put himself at risk, to make himself vulnerable and perhaps give his enemies (and both his faults and his success have gained him not a few) a chance of attacking him openly, or at least of whispering words to his detriment in the corridors of power. He needs to face his old bugbear, the fear of weakness, the fear of being no good, of being dependent on the good will and generosity of others. He needs to identify on a personal level with the weak, the failures, the unhappy, and to learn the lesson of St Paul, that Christ's strength is made perfect in weakness. If he fails to come to terms with this secret fear he will be forced to become more aloof and high handed in his attitude to others. He is likely to become lonely and embittered, for his arrogance will deprive him of friends and his action for others' good, will awaken the opposition of people whose feelings have been wounded by his lack of consideration.

Rachel, the self-righteous, the last of our four, has probably the most difficult lesson of all to learn. For behind the attitude of moral superiority which at great cost she has built up there lies a feeling of guilt, a deep seated and largely unconscious tendency to reject herself as basically bad. Though she is a religious woman and well instructed in Christian belief she has never really understood the meaning of forgiveness. Somehow she feels that in order to be acceptable to God she must live an exemplary life, she must earn forgiveness by her good actions. She has not grasped the central gospel truth that we do not earn forgiveness, it is given us free. God accepts us not because we are good but because he loves us. The realisation that we are accepted by God is not the reward of a well spent life but a gift bestowed at life's outset if only we have the luck or the grace to grasp it. It is not that good actions are of no account but that the motives prompting them are all important. The enlightened christian tries to live a good life not to earn God's acceptance but out of gratitude for having been accepted. This truth Rachel will not easily grasp. She may understand it intellectually, but habit will make it hard for her to appropriate it in depth. In the past she has avoided the company of people of easy morals, partly to escape contamination, partly because she distrusts her ability to avoid sin. One way in which she might learn what forgiveness means would be to go out of her way to associate with such people, to make friends with them, to learn to love them, to sympathize with their attitudes, share their troubles and vibrate with their humanity.

## THE RESOURCES OF THE GOSPEL

Our four characters have been so simplified, in order to illustrate common human problems, as to be caricatures. In dis-
cussing the last of them I have spoken explicitly about the
christian gospel and its bearing on the human condition. It is
time to look at the gospel more closely to see how its message
can help people both to discharge their human tasks and
realize themselves to the full. The force and universal
relevance of the gospel has been obscured by the way that it
has sometimes been presented, as though it concerned only the
especially religious or those who were prepared to become so.
But part of what the gospel declares is the loving action of God
towards all men, not only believers but unbelievers, not only
christians but atheistic communists. He is at work in all men
drawing them, persuading them towards wholeness, towards
the realisation of their humanity to the full, towards salvation.
But what God can do in and for men is limited, is conditioned
by men's own attitude. He helps all without exception who are
open to receive his help. What God has disclosed himself to be
in the life, death and rising again of Jesus Christ that he is
always and everywhere. What God has done for christians
through Jesus Christ is a uniquely important instance of what
he seeks to do for all men. What he does for those who open
themselves to him through their faith in Christ is what he is
seeking to do for all who without benefit of faith in Christ open
themselves to him. Noone is outside the range of God's loving
action and many respond to it and are enriched by it without
recognising the divine source of their blessings. The word that
denotes for christians the attitude by which men open
themselves to God's sustaining, life-enhancing action is faith.
Unfortunately the meaning of faith has often been narrowed
down to bare belief, or at least primarily to belief. But faith as
the New Testament understands it is a complex attitude including not only belief but a number of other attitudes
associated with it, preeminent among which is trust. These

qualities associated with belief and logically dependent on it are distinct from it and often exist without it. It is sometimes thought of as something of a scandal that many who profess no christian belief exhibit christian moral and spiritual qualities. I believe that these people despite having little or no belief do possess in marked degree some of these associate qualities.

The first of these qualities is trust. This was the aspect of faith most conspicuous in the teaching of Jesus. Those he taught took for granted the existence of God. What Jesus insisted on was that this belief must be expressed in trust. He expressed astonishment at men's unbelief and hardness of heart. It was not disbelief but unwillingness to trust that surprised him. He reproached his disciples for their mistrust. 'Why are you so fearful, O you of little faith.' Faith and fear are opposites. To be anxious and worried, especially about trivial things, is a practical denial either of God's goodness or his power. Jesus did not ignore the reality of evil nor suppose that putting complete trust in God was a guarantee of security from all the ills and dangers that beset mankind. He pointed to the birds as a picture of an unanxious, carefree life, and certainly their song and their free flight suggests a joyous delight in life. But birds sometimes freeze to death in winter and starve in time of drought. Jesus was well aware of his enemies who would eventually bring him to the cross and he warned his disciples to be ready for persecution. The trust that Jesus enjoined upon his disciples was no escape route from trouble. It was just the proper human response to God. Many children of good and sensible parents grow up with an attitude of basic trust towards other people, towards life, towards the world. It is God's gift to them through their parents. And despite harsh experiences many retain this basic trust through life. According to psychologists such as Erikson this fundamental trust is the indispensable foundation for growth towards self-realisation. It would seem overwhelmingly probable that Jesus from his earliest years was surrounded by a love that awakened and fostered this basic trust. He habitually addressed God, to the surprise and perhaps the scandal of his contemporaries, by the aramaic word, *Abba*, the word by which a very small child addressed his father, a word expressing intimate and affectionate trust.

Jesus was well aware that men were incapable of trusting God in the wholehearted way that he enjoined without abundant help from God. The gospel affirms not the duty of trusting God but the God-given ability to trust him. This ability is granted through the Holy Spirit who enters the lives of those who rely on Jesus Christ and releases in them the ability to trust. The Holy Spirit is the Spirit of sonship who, in St Paul's words, cries *Abba* in the hearts of disciples. Out of the depths of their being their flows an energy of trust which enables them to cast care aside and face difficulty and danger with an unanxious mind. They are brought into the same intimate relationship to God that Jesus had. How are we to distinguish the basic trust which is the bonus that comes from a good home and the trust which comes through Jesus Christ? Both are God's gift. Perhaps the theological axiom that grace both heals and perfects nature can help to make the distinction clear. The basic attitude of trust is a gift of nature, which some possess in abundance, others to a lesser degree, others hardly at all. Those who possess this basic trust will find that through Jesus Christ and the indwelling Spirit their trust will expand and deepen into an intimate reliance on God in all things. But those who lack this basic trust and are saddled with painful memories and emotional problems from the past, which handicap and perhaps cripple their development as persons, will need something more. They will look in addition for the healing of old emotional wounds and the building up of this fundamental attitude of trust towards life and people. This is what the gospel promises to those who will open themselves to it.

The second of the qualities or attitudes associated with belief is venture or commitment. It can be understood as the active counterpart of trust. It is putting trust in God to the test of action. An eminent example from the Bible of this aspect of faith is Abraham. In the ancient story Abraham's faith in God was tested by the summons to leave his ancestral home in Mesopotamia and set out across the desert to a destination unknown. Jesus summoned men to throw in their lot with him, to commit themselves to his cause. There is an element of venture of risktaking in faith. Jesus declared that the man who tried to save his life would lose it and the man who risked it for his sake and the Kingdom would gain it. Once he invited a rich man to sell all his property, give the proceeds away and throw in his lot with him. Until a person is prepared to act in faith, faith remains insubstantial and ineffective. Only decisive action can sever the rope that keeps faith grounded and permit it to become airborne. But just as trust in God has its natural counterpart in the basic trust that a person gains in childhood, so this venturing aspect of faith is paralleled by a natural spirit of adventure, a bold and positive attitude to people and events. This is one of the elements of ego strength which develops as hope and will and purpose grow in a child whose home life is favourable. The adventurous attitude to life, the willingness to confront danger and take risks is a human quality possessed by many who have little or no faith in God. I believe none the less that it is God's gift however unrecognised, a gift given through nature and nurture combined. Faith in God strengthens this quality and adds depth to it by linking it with an overall view of the meaning of life as finding its deepest significance in out and out commitment to the Kingdom.

There is a third element which together with trust and commitment combines to give strength and vitality to christian belief, experience. Faith has been called a kind of knowledge, an intuitive awareness of the unseen. Intuition has been defined as perception by way of the unconscious. To know by intuition is to know without being able to say how you know. This quality of faith adds conviction to bare belief. 'Faith makes us certain of realities we do not see'[2] It has been likened to the immediate knowledge of a person that comes from meeting and conversing with him in contrast to the knowledge about him gained from reading or hearsay. The discipline of the mystic or contemplative is designed to help focus the awareness of the transcendent reality that draws him and to enable him to enter into closer communion with it. Though the christian mystics have nearly all been orthodox believers the experience they describe is of a 'dark knowledge', of an 'unknowing'. Their belief enables them to interpret their experience and their experience colours their belief with the hue of certainty. But the mystical experience does not appear to depend on christian belief, for those of other faiths and of none have described experiences strikingly similar to those of the

orthodox christian mystic. Many also who would not be
thought of as mystics have known the experience, described by
Wordsworth in immortal lines, of:

A presence that disturbs me with the joy
Of elevated thoughts: a sense sublime
Of something far more deeply interfused
Whose dwelling is the light of setting suns,
And the round ocean and the living air
And the blue sky, and in the mind of man.[3]

This sense of 'something more' whether in the contemplation
of nature or of human life is felt by many who have no definite
religious belief and, when experienced by believers, is
sometimes not seen as connected with their belief. It seems
that there is a natural experience of the transcendent, as there
is a natural spirit of trust and a natural spirit of commitment
to an unknown. Each of these attitudes is a response, whether
realised as such or not, to the unseen God who is present
within all men without exception. The christian's faith is no
substitute for these attitudes. Rather it should complete or
heal or help to develop them by integrating them with a
response to what God has said and is saying through Jesus
Christ.

Faith is a complex attitude including four elements, of
which belief is only one. I believe that a large part of the
difficulty many sympathetic moderns have with Christianity is
the difficulty of accepting christian belief or doctrine understood in isolation from the three elements associated with it,
the elements which give it power and vitality. Christian
doctrine has been presented too often as a set of abstract
statements. It is as though when you are hoping to see a man
you are shown a skeleton. No wonder people are put off. The
statements of the creed are not the objects of our belief but
signposts pointing to an Unknown. I believe they are reliable
signposts, but the object of belief is God who altogether
transcends our knowing. We know him in part, but our ignorance immensely outweighs our knowledge. We know him
as a child knows the ocean after a single visit to the seaside. He
knows the look of the sea from the shore, he knows the feel of

water washing against his legs when paddling, he knows the salt taste of the sea. But he doesn't know the ocean, its vast extent, its teeming life, the contours of the ocean bed, its tides, its storms and its currents. So we know God and we don't know him. But though we know him so little we can trust him, we can commit ourselves to him, we can respond to the intimations of glory and majesty with which he visits us.

We have been considering in this chapter the tasks of adult life. They can be seen as the necessary means by which we develop our humanity to the utmost of its capacity, by which we live out our own truth to the full and pay our debts to the society which has nourished us. They can equally be understood as a summons to respond to the Creator, whose love has all our life been searching for means to set us free from the hindrances to self-realisation, who is telling us not only to discharge our responsibilities as citizens and friends, perhaps as artists or craftsmen, perhaps as parents, but also to prepare ourselves for a destiny beyond this world. Faith is the attitude or the set of inter-related attitudes by which we respond to God who alone can enable us to discharge these responsibilities and fulfil this destiny. This attitude of faith is God's gift for which there is no substitute. But it is a gift that he desires to give; indeed he has given to all men in germ the capacity to respond to him. How can this God-given capacity be developed? Principally by prayer understood in its widest sense. Prayer educates, expands and deepens faith. This will be the subject of the next four chapters.

1. Op. cit. p. 26.
2. Hebrews 11,1.
3. Lines composed above Tintern Abbey.

# 6. The Presence of God

and prayer is more
Than an order of words, the conscious occupation
Of the praying mind, or the sound of the voice praying.
                                    T.S. Eliot, *Little Gidding* ll.46–48

Persons who have little conscious belief in God sometimes confront life, other people, the future with a trust and commitment which seem to imply reliance on God. Such unconscious reliance on God is probably the result of their fortunate upbringing; they are responding to God without knowing it. For them prayer will be a focusing, a making fully conscious and explicit, of the unconscious prayer that their life implies. They will find that praying consciously and deliberately will bring to their whole way of life a greater coherence, direction and strength. But there are a great many who do pray regularly yet whose attitude to life is deficient in trust and commitment. This may well be a legacy from the past for which they are not to blame. For them however it will be important so to deepen and broaden their praying that it will infuse into all their activities and relationships the attitude of reliance on God which they express verbally when they pray.

# THE APPROACH TO GOD

There is a two way relationship between prayer and life. Prayer can be seen as the focusing and redirecting of an attitude to God and to our fellows that runs through all that we do. On the other hand we can see our daily life as something which prayer purifies, directs and consecrates. This interrelationship of prayer and life was expressed by William Temple in his well known saying 'It is not that conduct is the end of life and worship helps it but that worship is the end of life and conduct tests it.' Temple is here using worship in a broad sense to include all of life. For in worship, as the derivation of the word from worth implies, we declare what we value most. If in prayer I declare that I value God above all things and in my life I show that my own selfish interests come first I am making a nonsense of my praying. We declare how we value God as much by our actions, by the way we treat other people, by the manner in which we do our work, as by anything we say. If my actions are wrong or wrongly motivated prayer cannot make them right. If however, despite my failures and inconsistencies, I do on the whole want to put God above all things then prayer will help to purify my motives and clarify my judgment.

Perhaps the commonest difficulty felt about prayer is the sense of unreality that can invest the whole transaction. This may be partly due to an inconsistency between what I affirm in prayer and the whole tenor and direction of my life. In so far as this is so only amendment of life will bring reality into my prayer. But over and above the difficulty caused by the clash between actions and profession there is an obvious difficulty in entering into a conscious relationship with one who is invisible and who does not speak in any unmistakable way. For this reason the spiritual guides insist on the importance at the very outset of prayer of trying to realize God's presence, or of making an act of faith in God. This exercise, sometimes described as 'placing yourself in the presence of God', is not as simple as it is sometimes made to sound. In this chapter I want to reflect on what realizing God's presence means and to suggest how this focusing on God may best be done.

First, the realisation of God, the awareness of him, is one of the elements of a living faith and is a gift of God. Only God himself can elicit it. Faith is a response to God which if it is genuine must involve commitment and trust. It may be that the reason why I do not realize God's presence is that I am shrinking from personal commitment to him. My relationship to God resembles my relationship to my mother. Though I may have become estranged from my mother, nothing can alter the fact that she is the mother who bore me, who fed and cared for me in my infancy. Just so God is my Author, one who is intimately related to me whether I will it or no. To be aware of God must be to be aware of him as my God, the God whose power and wisdom sustains me in existence. To be aware of one as intimate to me and as demanding as God, is perhaps more than I really want. Perhaps this is the greatest of all the obstacles to the realisation of God's presence, the fact that we only want it half-heartedly and that a strong consciousness of God's presence might be much more than we had bargained for.

There are two complementary ways of approaching the unseen God. Both are needed but some approach predominantly by the one road, some by the other. Charles Williams has called these two approaches the way of affirmation and the way of negation. They might be summarised by the two antithetical statements: *this also is Thou* and *neither is this Thou*. God is present in all persons and in all happenings, and it is possible to salute God in everything that touches our life: this also is Thou. But having said that we have to call to mind the opposite truth, that God transcends our understanding and that to identify him simply with any event or person is to belittle the uncreated Godhead and reduce God in thought to the level of a creature: neither is this Thou. On the whole the affirmative way, the way that sees God reflected in the created world, is the way nearly everyone begins; some people follow that way all their lives. The negative way becomes more important as we grow older; it is the typical way of the contemplative or mystic.

It would seem right that our way of prayer should follow the grain of our growth from childhood through adolescence to adulthood. During childhood and youth, as we have seen, one of the important tasks is to acquire a certain strength of character, 'ego-strength', which will enable us to manage our biological drives without repressing them and to confront and to make our own individual response to the influences and expectations of society. The prayer that recognises God's presence in the world of people and events around us will foster the courage to overcome undue diffidence in the face of older people and established custom. Later as we become more assured in our work and home, among our friends and in the larger social world we shall need to learn the lessons of the negative way, that God's ways are not our ways nor his thoughts our thoughts, that friendship with the world means enmity with God, that he is the Unknown and must be approached by the way of ignorance.

In beginning to reflect on the affirmative way whose motto is 'this also is Thou', I believe it is important to understand God's presence dynamically, as an active presence, or, to put it another way, that God is present where he acts. To say that God is present everywhere is to say that God is acting everywhere. Like the sun whose rays radiate outwards in every direction making life possible on the earth, the rays of God's action and influence sustain everything in being from the largest of the giant stars to the tiniest neutron, from the trees of the forest to the fish in the ocean, from the lowly earth worm to man, made in God's image. The presssure of God's influence on each item of creation is towards its being itself and fulfilling its potential to the utmost of its capacity. In the case of man God's influence fosters his growth to human maturity, to full personhood, to responsibility for his actions and concern for his fellows. God acts on each and all of us through the world in which we live, through the people we meet, through our work and leisure, through our thinking and planning, through our dreams and through the unaccountable thoughts and impulses that push their way into consciousness. Because God treats us as persons and will never violate our freedom, he waits for us to open ourselves to him and cannot force his way into our hearts. In prayer we turn to face the silent pressure of 'the inexhaustible power for good and the inexhaustible fund of invention and contrivance.'

## THE SIGNS OF GOD'S PRESENCE

God acts upon us and influences us through everything that is and everything that happens, but some things speak more eloquently of God than others, some objects and events are signs which seem to point unmistakably to God. One approach to realising God's presence is to reflect upon these signs, to listen to what God is saying through them, to look through the signs towards the God who speaks to us in them. The prayer which best expresses and fosters the realisation of God is the prayer of adoration. This is a God-centred prayer in which the thought of ourselves is reduced to a minimum. In the prayer of petition we are conscious of our needs, in thanksgiving of our blessings, in confession of our sins, but in adoration we acknowledge God without thought of ourselves. We respond in adoration to supreme Reality, to overflowing Goodness, to uncreated Beauty. You are driving, let us say, in the Highlands of Scotland, you turn a corner and there spreading out before you is a superb view, an expanse of water and, rising up behind it, a heather clad mountain and on the further horizon a range of mountain peaks. You give a gasp of delight, the lovely loch with its backdrop of mountain compels your response. In adoration we exclaim with awe and wonder at the sheer fact of God. We all want truth, reality; noone is happy to live in a fool's paradise. God is the Reality behind all that is real, who alone can slake the metaphysical thirst for truth. In adoration we acknowledge ultimate reality. There is thus an affinity between adoration and the sciences. The scientist regards the facts of his science as sacred and not to be tampered with. The plot of C.P. Snow's novel *The Affair* turns on the allegation that the research fellow of a Cambridge college has committed the cardinal sin of faking a photograph to provide evidence in support of a scientific thesis. The scientists in the novel are outraged at the possibility of such an action. The scientist who discovers some new fact about the structure of the atom or the chemistry of the brain experiences a thrill which is akin to adoration. But science is less concerned about truth than about truths. It limits itself to the task of discovering truths about particular regions of reality; and within those regions it concentrates on what it can measure and map. And so the truth of science is the truth of a map. It bears the same kind of relation to the reality it is concerned with as a map has to the country it charts. A map for all its usefulness to the traveller cannot give him the same kind of knowledge of a country that he gains from visiting and exploring it for himself. Science is engaged in making more and more accurate and extensive maps of the universe. It will never be able to tell us the things that cannot be described on a map. The signs by which God addresses us are not the abstractions of science but the concrete objects, events and persons that touch our lives. Nevertheless the scientific maps if only we realize what they can do for us can greatly help our adoration, for if we will learn from them they will illuminate our understanding and sharpen our vision of the objects through which God addresses us. They help to awaken the wonder which is part of the spirit of adoration.

Another of the signs which can point a person to God and lead him into adoration is goodness as he meets it in his fellow men and women. There is a profound instinct to give honour where honour is due. Outstanding courage or generosity or self-sacrifice moves us deeply; it awakens in us the sense that that is the way a person should act, the way that we ourselves would like to act if only we could master the fears that inhibit action. The honour we instinctively pay to goodness is the affirmation of value, it is a kind of worship, it is the seed of the worship that we pay to God, the author and inspirer of all real goodness. The christian who acknowledges that God has spoken to mankind uniquely in Jesus Christ will be able to see in the heroism and self-sacrifice of the cross a kind of central pattern into which all lesser acts of goodness can fit. And the greatest of all christian acts of adoration is a setting forth in word and symbolic rite of that death that took place 1900 years ago.

A further sign which can point us to the invisible Godhead, too little regarded by christians in the past, is beauty; or rather not abstract beauty but the beautiful sights and sounds that woo our senses. Aquinas defines beauty as *id quod visum placet*, that which delights you when you see it. Beauty awakens joy. It summons the believer to rejoice in God, 'in whose presence is the fullness of joy.' All objects of beauty can be understood

as heralds sent by God to summon us to joy. Beauty can
indeed be terrible. For lightning at night, the mountainous
waves of a storm at sea, the vast bulk of an iceberg glittering in
the sun, can awaken a thrill of delight even though they arouse
a quiver of fear. The uncreated beauty which is God must fill
us with awe even while it attracts us irresistibly. Beauty disturbs and threatens us; it awakens a delight that is fleeting and
prophesies a joy that will last. Christians have tended to be
suspicious of beauty and it is easy to understand why. For the
beauty that delights us can lead us into a kind of idolatry; we
can be betrayed into worshipping the King's herald and
forgetting the King he is announcing. St Augustine himself
was afraid of beautiful music in worship lest it encouraged an
aestheticism which would divert men from God to the music
which was meant to lead them to him. But despite the
authority of St Augustine who was suspicious of the body and
pleasure, we need beauty in worship to enlist in the adoration
of God a region of our being that would otherwise be excluded.
The beauty of music and ceremony bring a richness and
delight that can enlarge our apprehension of the Unknown
and Invisible whom we adore. It can give wings to that aspect
of adoration which we call praise. For there are two complementary movements in the worship of God, both of which
are aspects of adoration, adoration in the narrow sense and
praise. In adoration I affirm the supreme greatness of God and
my nothingness by comparison; in praise I exult in God and
feel myself twice the man I am because God is God. Worship
both exalts and abases; adoration and praise are the opposite
sides of a single coin. Beauty especially invites us to rejoice in
God. There is a way of looking at or listening to beautiful
sights and sounds that leads us into the presence of God.

It is not abstract truth, beauty and goodness that speak to
us of God but their embodiment in concrete objects and actual
happenings. Of all the concrete objects by means of which
God speaks home to us the commonest and most effective are
our fellow human beings, the living, breathing images of God.
When Dante first set eyes on Beatrice he saw in her his bliss,
his salvation, he saw Christ. Being a great poet he was led by
this vision to write the *Divine Comedy*. Charles Williams in his
*Figure of Beatrice*[1] has expounded that poem as the working out

in the light of his christian belief of the meaning of the splendour which unmade and remade him, the light which shone in
the eyes of that Florentine girl. We who lack Dante's poetic
genius but possess his Christian faith can learn something of
what God is saying to us if we reflect on the personalities of
those who make an impact upon us. There are two sorts of
person in particular through whom God addresses us, those
who especially attract us and those who repel.

Consider first of all those who attract us. If I am a somewhat
timid person I may feel strongly drawn to someone who seems
to breathe out force, boldness and courage. He attracts me
because he arouses my own dormant capacity to act without
fear. God seeks through him to arouse part of my manhood.
Such a person focuses for me an awareness both of God and of
myself. Or again I may be excessively cautious and buttoned
up in my attitude to people, afraid of giving myself away and
making myself appear ridiculous. I find myself much drawn to
someone who is just the opposite, who is outgoing and spontaneous in his attitude to others, who says what he feels
regardless of what he may look like. I find him refreshing and
liberating because he begins to release in me my own
neglected capacity to be spontaneous and natural. He is for me
a messenger of God and a minister of grace. Or, to take
another instance, I have a fear of being dependent on others, a
legacy from my struggle to escape from undue dependence on
my parents in early childhood. I am inclined to keep myself to
myself and especially to avoid taking anyone into my confidence about my problems. I will face and solve these on my
own or not at all. Then I meet someone who fascinates me
because he, or it may well be she, seems to be completely
devoid of my stand-offishness, who finds it entirely natural to
seek advice from others, to share problems and receive help. I
am attracted because he represents a quality that I need; he
helps to free me from my self-chosen isolation; God speaks
powerfully and persuasively to me through his personality.
Such persons as these may influence me for good whether or
not I recognise them as sent by God. But if I am able to see
God in them the message that they embody will carry greater
weight and my awareness of God's presence, action and influence will be strengthened and enlarged.

What of those who repel me? God addresses me through them in warning and judgment. If I am a slightly different person the very same people who now attract me will put me off, will make me feel embarrassed and ill at ease. For example, a person whose forthright attitude to people speaks home to my capacity to act boldly threatens my ideal of myself as a quiet, unobtrusive person, who keeps himself in the background. He threatens to arouse the sleeping dog of my natural aggressiveness, which I am afraid of and have kept firmly repressed. He will appear to me to be the type of person I most dislike. He will in fact be a God-sent rebuke to my undue timidity, my cowardly evasion of responsibility. He represents an element in myself that I am rejecting and also the God who is warning me through him that I am refusing life. Again, if, through some painful experience of rejection in childhood when my affection was rebuffed, I am afraid of my affectionateness and keep it imprisoned behind a cold and aloof manner, then someone who arouses it is likely to make me feel anxious and uncertain of myself. The warmheartedness of such a person will threaten my aloofness and may lead me to redouble my defences, perhaps by means of an icy politeness which keeps him or her at a distance. Or, suppose my defensiveness is due to a strongly repressed tendency to be over-dependent on others, then the man or woman of kindly and helpful disposition may strike me as intolerably interfering or patronising, because his personality tends to undermine my inner defences. He will in truth be a messenger from God warning me to repent, to stop rejecting the undeveloped child in myself, to face its immaturity and allow it into the daylight of consciousness where it will change and grow up. Other sorts of person will repel me for similar reasons. One person irritates me because he strikes me as overconscientious, and so arouses my uneasy conscience. Another fills me with distaste because he seems eaten up with self-pity and so sets throbbing the inner wound of my own self-pity which I hate and despise. Through those who repel us God, I believe, often challenges us to face and come to terms with rejected bits of ourselves which we have been repudiating. Through such unwelcome signs God summons us to repent, to change, to face openly what we are, to live our own truth. He

will not leave me in peace if I try to evade the truth of what I
am and bury my God-given talent in the ground.

## REALISING GOD'S PRESENCE

God acts upon us inescapably through the people who touch
and influence our lives. Whatever our belief or disbelief these
influences cannot be questioned. If I do not believe in God I
shall not see him behind these influences but I shall be subject
to them none the less. If I do believe in God my wisdom will be
to learn to recognize him addressing me in mercy and
judgment through my fellows. But most of us will only be able
to recognize his presence here after prolonged reflection. One
of the surest methods of learning through reflection to focus
the attention on God is the discipline of *lectio divina*, spiritual
reading.

At a time when books are mass produced and the typical
reader races through one book in order to begin another the
name spiritual reading may easily deceive a person as to the
nature of this exercise. It is much more like meditation or
prayer than the reading of a book as this is normally understood. It is a slow, reflective reading with frequent pauses. It is
reading with the attention deliberately divided and working on
different levels. The reader searches for the meaning that the
writer intended, he uses his imagination to recreate the scenes
and the persons described, he tries to follow the author's
reasoning, to enter into his mind. He is listening to a fellow
human being who may have lived two thousand years ago. But
all the time he is attending to something else. He is looking for
and listening to the words, the phrases, the names of power,
the images that echo and reverberate deep within. He is listening to the emotions aroused, the inner echoes, the spiritual intuitions, the aspirations towards God that start up from the
deep places of the heart. And when the flame of aspiration is
kindled he pushes his book aside, he holds himself still and
attentive, he lets the flame burn as long as it will. He is using
reading as a way of approaching God, of making himself
aware of God. For myself, who at other times like to read
rapidly, I find that I do spiritual reading best with pen and

paper beside me to write down what strikes me. Writing checks haste which is the enemy of real reflection. It also records the words and phrases which opened the locked door to my depths. To reread the phrases, the metaphors, the compelling images is often an effective way of reopening the door, of recovering the awareness or the insight that the words originally awakened.

Spiritual reading is a reading which helps us to focus our attention on God's presence within, in the soul's centre. The Eastern Orthodox spiritual tradition describes this inner focusing as 'holding the mind in the heart'. Many different kinds of book may be found useful and in fact the manner of reading is more important than the actual book read. Each individual must search for the book that opens the way to his own depths, whether it be a well known spiritual classic, some modern work or just the Bible. Pride of place must be given by the christian to Holy Scripture, despite the difficulties of interpretation; and within Scripture the psalms from the Old Testament and the gospels from the New are the books that are the most likely sources of inspiration. The way to read Scripture is not only to ponder the meaning of the words and to recreate in imagination the scenes described but to listen to the Word, to God himself speaking in the heart. We perceive his action within by a certain inner quickening of interest, a heightened awareness, a sudden illumination, an inflow of peace, a leap of joy. Sometimes what I experience is not peace but a sword, my conscience is disturbed, I become aware of some wrong motive or action or some action left undone, I am granted some painful piece of self-knowledge.

Many people find the reading of the gospel story in this manner an effective means of leading the mind into the heart. St Teresa of Avila used to picture the incidents of the life of Christ as taking place in her heart. Her attention moved between the scene she pictured and the presence within her heart that no thought could grasp. The event from the past, recreated in her imagination, was the medium through which she focused her attention on God in the present. The historic actuality to which the gospel points lit up the actuality of God's presence within her.

Jung's method of active imagination can usefully be adapted

to prayer. The method was designed to help a person to become more aware of and open to the unconscious. He was encouraged to recall and concentrate on the mental image of some impressive figure, whether occurring in a dream, in a waking fantasy or in every day life. He would then in imagination question the figure and in an attitude of relaxed attentiveness, wait for the answer that comes into his mind. The exercise is one of imagination; there is nothing necessarily profound or wise in the answers; they merely offer a point of view worth considering. Something like this exercise could be applied to the gospel stories. Take, for example, the account of Jesus healing a leper given in Mark chapter one. You see in imagination the leper coming and throwing himself at the feet of Jesus; you hear him speak, 'Lord, if you will you can make me clean.' You see the indignation on the face of Jesus, you watch him lean forward and put his hands on the leper's head, you hear the words, 'I will, be thou clean'. And then you watch the change from sickness to health, from depression to joy and hope. So far you have been trying to imagine the scene, but now you enter into it more actively. You not only picture what happens, you address one or other of the actors in the scene. For example you ask the healed leper how he feels or what he thinks of Jesus, and then you wait for something in you to suggest his answer. What is the aim of such an exercise? Not to discover anything new but through the power of imagination to activate a knowledge and trust which deep down you possess. Those of vivid imagination will have no difficulty over the picturing. The unimaginative need not be deterred if they can only picture vaguely a figure of strength and compassion and a figure of extreme need. Either image may speak with power to your depths and enable you to realize at a deeper level both your own profound need and the healing power of Christ. Those who use their imagination in this way must remember that no picture or idea can adequately represent God. Thought and imagination can prepare me for prayer but I have to leave them behind when I actually turn to God. For though God is present within us he is not to be identified with any idea, image, feeling or sensation. Such may indeed be signs pointing to him but to identify God with them is to fall into a kind of idolatry. God is greater than anything we can think or imagine. We can name him but we cannot grasp him.

Words can help the realization of God's presence in two different ways. They can help to focus an idea or image in my mind and they can help me to look through or away from the idea to the unknown Presence that the idea points to. Take the words of the Jesus prayer, familiar now not only in its home in the Eastern Orthodox Church but throughout the West: 'Lord Jesus Christ, Son of God, have mercy upon me.' I can begin by using the words to concentrate my attention, first on the great names of Christ – Jesus, Christ, Son of God – and then on our human frailty in body, mind and spirit and our great need of divine compassion. The words repeated slowly many times help these truths to penetrate from the head to the heart. But after some time I begin to say the words differently. I no longer try to enter into the meaning of the words. I know what they mean but I don't think what they mean. Instead I attend to a presence in my heart, it is as though a flame of aspiration kindles there, a yearning towards an indwelling companion whom I trust and love.

Many people are content with the Jesus prayer for all occasions like the Russian pilgrim in the *Way of a Pilgrim*.[2] But many will want more variety. For myself I have found psalm verses a great help to focusing my attention on God, not whole psalms but specially selected verses. 'Be still then and know that I am God.'[3] 'Out of the deep have I called unto thee O Lord: Lord hear my voice.'[4] 'Like as the hart desireth the waterbrooks so longeth my soul after thee O God.'[5] 'O send out thy light and thy truth that they may lead me.'[6] These verses from the psalms can be used in the same way as the Jesus prayer. First we think out what we intend by the words, then we repeat the words many times slowly so as to let the meaning sink right in, and then we continue saying the words without thinking of the meaning, but rather waiting on God, letting the flame of aspiration burn in the heart without deliberate or concentrated thinking. I have often found it a help to repeat either the Jesus prayer or a phrase from the psalms while fingering beads on a rosary. The passing from bead to bead helps to keep out distraction and help concentration. I have found this especially helpful when I have left off thinking about the words and am attending directly to God. The pressure of the fingers on the beads helps to keep my aspirations focused on him.

The mention of the rosary is a reminder of the important part the body can play in supporting the concentration of the mind. Stillness of body helps concentration of mind. Many in the West are learning that the techniques of Yoga, especially the breathing methods and the simpler postures, greatly assist the physical stillness and relaxation that helps concentration. Further, in the act of adoration which is an appropriate prelude to prayer the body can play a valuable part. By prostrating myself – that is by kneeling (or lying prostrate) with forehead resting on the floor – I find that I am more completely involved in worship. Many a christian, I fancy, who while professing to believe firmly in God seldom or never has any awareness of his presence, would begin to gain this awareness if he would regularly make this act of bodily obeisance, saying slowly the words of the Sanctus or the phrase from the Psalm (95.6) 'O come let us worship and fall down and kneel before the Lord our Maker.' The act of prostration, like the act of kissing or embracing, is part of the age-old language of the body and expresses a meaning that cannot be wholly put into words.

Before concluding this chapter about realising God's presence it is necessary to refer to the disconcerting and paradoxical fact that those who begin to take their religion seriously commonly go through a period, sometimes a long period, when they experience the apparent absence of God. The ideas, images, concepts which they have previously used in thinking about God or addressing him have suddenly become meaningless and unreal. The person feels as if God is absent or does not exist. The reason for this disagreeable phenomenon is that while the intuition is seeking for a deeper, more genuine knowledge of God, psychic energy is drawn away from consciously held beliefs and ideas towards a dark knowledge, a knowledge of the heart, an awareness of God speaking through the deep centre. It is the action of God himself in an unexpected and unfamiliar mode that makes him seem absent. The difficulty is made more formidable from the fact that God is most surely to be found close to those areas of

ourselves that have been repressed and shut away from consciousness. The four imaginary characters of the previous two
chapters will serve to illustrate what happens.

Let us suppose that each of our four has some formal
religion and then in adult life decides to give religion high
priority. Let us consider what is likely to happen. Samuel's
personal ideal for himself is of one who tries hard to maintain a
tranquil mind in all circumstances. One of the reasons for this
is the desire to banish from his mind the memory of his
childhood terrors. His idea of God is likely to give prominence
to the peace and tranquillity of the Godhead, for this aspect of
God fits in best with his ideal and will help to repress his
memories of fear. But now that he has made up his mind to
put God first in his life his old idea of God begins to seem unreal. He has to learn that the true God is leading him to face
the situations he has been evading. He will rediscover God's
presence in a more genuine way than ever before as he begins
to face his fears and to turn to God not as a refuge from fear
but as a power that will enable him to overcome it.

The experience of the other three is likely to be similar to
Samuel's. Nancy's ideal of being nice to everyone and so winn-
ing their affection is partly rooted in an unconscious fear of rejection. Her idea of God is likely to be of one who is all-kind
and to leave out the sterner aspects of the Godhead. When she
begins to take God seriously and not merely as a support to
her ideal she is shattered to find that her old idea of God seems
meaningless. She has to learn to find him anew as she
struggles to face her fear of rejection and the insincerity into
which it has led her. Peter's ideal of himself as a fighter for the
Kingdom is too much powered by a repressed but still active
fear of failure. His idea of God will probably be of the God of
battles who will help him in his battle for righteousness. As he
begins to realize the true character of God's Kingdom he is
likely to find that his old concept of God evaporates. He will be
forced to face the possibility of failure and to find God as the
Succour of the weak. Rachel, the last of our four, has to learn
that God will not help her to maintain her self-righteous image
of her self and her idea of him as loving only those who are
good. And if she genuinely seeks his will this idea of him,
which she had relied on to help repress her feeling of guilt, will

fade into unreality. She will be led to face her guilt feelings and let them be withered up in the measureless love of God, who forgives our sin and heals our infirmity.

As I pointed out in an earlier chapter the characters I have sketched are caricatures. Real people are mysterious and complex and cannot be summed up in a few sentences without gross distortion. The sketches are designed to illustrate in diagramatic form the nature of the experience of God's absence and the part it plays in spiritual growth. From ignorance of what is happening to them when they try to serve God more sincerely people are often much cast down and sometimes give up their purpose in despair. The experience of the absence of God is an unsought initiation into the negative way of approaching God, the way in which we progress by renouncing what we think we know about God and following a way of ignorance or unknowing. But we shall have to look more closely at this way in a later chapter, when we consider mysticism and contemplative prayer.

1. Faber and Faber 1943.
2. SPCK 1972, with an introduction by Archbishop Anthony Bloom
3. Psalm 46, 10.
4. Psalm 130, 1.
5. Psalm 42, 1.
6. Psalm 43.3.

# 7. The Hope of the Kingdom

And all shall be well and
All manner of things shall be well
By the purification of the motive
In the ground of our beseeching.

T.S. Eliot, *Little Gidding* ll.156–159

It comes as something of a shock to some twentieth century Christians, interested in meditation and contemplation and ready to turn to Eastern gurus for instruction in these arts, to learn that in his teaching about prayer Jesus assumes that prayer means petition to God. 'Ask and you shall receive'. 'Men ought always to pray and not to lose heart.' 'Pray for your enemies.' The pattern prayer he gave to his disciples consists of seven petitions. One reason for the modern revulsion against petitionary prayer may be its association with the childish superstitious prayers that are sometimes made. But I believe the principal reason is a weakened sense of the reality of God and of his active presence everywhere. This Jesus took for granted; and he could assume that his hearers would also accept this in theory however much they might forget it in practice. We who live in a very different world from first century Palestine need to give time to meditating on God's presence and action before the prayer of petition will be seen as relevant and important. Before turning to the teaching of Jesus about prayer let us reflect briefly on the reasons for the prayer of petition.

# THE MEANING OF PETITIONARY PRAYER

That profound and sophisticated thinker of the thirteenth century Thomas Aquinas gave two reasons for petitionary prayer. To cooperate with divine providence and to awaken our confidence in him. Prayer is a means of working with divine Providence. When I pray I am not asking God to bring about my will but to bring about his. To the question 'Will not God bring about his will anyway whether I ask or not?' the answer is that there are some things that God will not bring about unasked and uninvited. God knocks at the door of our lives, he does not force his way in. By my petition I invite God in to bring about his will in ways that I cannot predict. Aquinas's second reason for the prayer of petition is to awaken our confidence in God. By treating God as a child treats his father I grow in a filial attitude to God, I come to trust him more. This attitude of confident trust that God is able and willing to help in ways which we cannot either foresee or fathom deepens our relationship to him. Petitionary prayer may in form be an unsophisticated type of prayer suitable to children and the uneducated, but it embodies deep psychological wisdom. For below the level of the sophisticated rational consciousness of the educated man of today there flows a largely unconscious but powerful current of emotion which influences him far more than he is aware. If his prayer is to be realised as meaningful these emotional depths must be involved. The value of simple and childlike language, especially if it contains vivid imagery, is that it elicits a response from his depths which he cannot otherwise obtain. The child which we once were, with its fears and its capacity for trust, lives on in us and needs to participate in our prayer if the prayer is not to seem superficial. And the prayer of petition does express a truth that the most sophisticated believer acknowledges, his total dependence on his Creator and Father.

The prayer of petition is an expression of trust in the living God, who is both Creator and Redeemer. God's action as Creator and his action as Redeemer flow from one simple and undivided will and purpose. But, though this unity of God's will must never be forgotten, it helps us to think clearly about it if we speak of God's action through nature and his action by grace. In an earlier chapter I spoke of basic trust which is God's gift to a child through the medium of his parents and home, God's gift through nature. This trust is itself a kind of inarticulate prayer even though God is not specifically named. Fully christian prayer, though it could and should include this basic trust learnt in childhood, will mean entering into a conscious and deliberately sought relationship of trust which will bring about changes in him and through him in others which will go beyond anything which can be accounted for in terms of nature or God's action through nature. Though harmonious with nature God's action by grace transforms men and women into sons and daughters of God, seeking a goal and responding to a presence that totally transcends this world. This becomes clearer when we look at Christ's teaching about prayer, illustrated so far as possible by his actual practice.

Let us begin by looking at one of the startling sayings of Jesus about prayer, a real stumbling block to the literal minded. 'If you ask anything of God believe that you have it and it shall be done unto you.'[1] Plainly he cannot mean that if only we can convince ourselves that God will bring something about then God will be forced to honour our convictions. Jesus often used to arrest his hearers' attention by stating a truth in exaggerated or unexpected language. What truth is he here trying to drive home by this paradoxical affirmation? Clearly he is telling us that we should pray with great confidence. I believe he is also telling us to use our imagination. 'Expect an answer to your prayer. Picture the thing asked for as already granted.' We must understand this saying in the context of his teaching about the necessity of faith, if we are to receive blessings which God wishes to give us, and the paralysing obstacle of unbelief and cynicism. God is waiting to pour immense blessings on those who will rely firmly on him, but everywhere he is met with a corporate unbelief, mistrust and selfish anxiety, which create an atmosphere that stifles the personal faith of individuals. Jesus is here telling his disciples to challenge the miasma of unbelief by means of faith-inspired imagination. . . 'When you pray get ready for an answer, picture how it would be if God took you at your word. God can bring about more than you suppose.' No doubt we are incapable of imagining with any precision the answers that God will give; we are too ignorant and there are too many imponderables. But the effort to imagine helps to dissipate the mistrust within ourselves, which would otherwise undermine our reliance on God. And though God does not make things happen the way we picture he may bring about its equivalent or something far better.

It is one thing to suppose that those who pray with this confident expectation will receive incalculable blessings. Can we feel the same assurance that others will equally be blessed in answer to the prayer of faith? Much new knowledge is reinforcing the old belief in the solidarity of mankind, the mutual and many-levelled interaction of men and women. Those who have investigated the evidence for extra-sensory perception – telepathy, clairvoyance and the phenomena which attend spiritualistic seances – have built up massive support for the conviction that everywhere mind flows into mind, that individuals are not wholly separate from each other but are unconsciously linked together. Like islands of an archipelago, joined together underneath the sea that separates them, we are knit together by invisible and unconscious ties. Spiritual blessings cannot be privatized, they are communal; and the attempt to turn them into a purely individual possession tends to destroy them. The petitions of the Lord's prayer are made in the first person plural.

The mental acts of which prayer consists are not purely mental. In proportion as they are sincere they must flow out of heart and will in harmony with the prayer and must issue in action in line with it where action is possible or appropriate. The old saying, 'sow a thought, reap an act; sow an act, reap a habit' and so forth, applies to the thoughts which are sown in prayer. The God-directed, God-relying thoughts which are part of genuine prayer will issue in God-directed, God-relying actions and habits. The prayer which opens a door into human life through which grace and mercy can flow is no mere mental gymnastic or exercise in thought control. It is a strong and purposeful aspiration which rises out of a mind and heart deeply committed to God and his reign. 'Whatsoever you shall ask the Father in my name he will give it you'[2] says Jesus to his disciples. To ask in Christ's name is much more than a matter of words, it is a prayer in harmony with the whole tenor and direction of Christ's life. The attitude to life which corresponds with the expectant prayer that Christ commends is the spirit of venture and especially venture for the kingdom. It is like the spirit of a man who finding treasure in a field buries it again and for sheer joy sells everything he has and buys the field; or like a dealer in precious stones who coming across a pearl of unique value realizes all his assets and buys it. Jesus states the principle even more starkly when he declares 'Whoever cares for his own safety is lost; but if a man will let himself be lost for my sake and for the gospel, that man is safe.'[3] The prayer that God's will may be done, as Jesus understands it, is not a prayer of passive resignation in the spirit of what must be must be. It is a prayer of confident expectation backed by a life committed to God's will and reign. There is a Jewish legend that when pursued by the Egyptian army the children of Israel came to the Red Sea the waters did not actually roll back until one Jewish man in an act of faith strode into the water. Only then did the path across the sea bed open up. The kind of prayer that Jesus teaches his disciples is expectant petition that God will in his own way intervene backed up by action which takes God's intervention for granted.

## PRAYER AND THE CONFRONTATION WITH EVIL

Let us try to understand Christ's prayer in Gethsemane in the light of this teaching. The first part of the prayer, 'suffer this cup to pass from me,'[4] expresses his shrinking from the appalling death by crucifixion that seems to confront him. There is no pretence of being indifferent to pain, no attempt to repress the revulsion of his manhood from such an end. And then in the second part of the prayer he prays, 'Nevertheless, thy will be done.' He utters the prayer out of a heart and will totally committed to the Father and confident that the Father will bring about his will in his own way. From Gethsemane he steps out to face the soldiers sent to arrest him and to meet his fate at the hands of hostile men. Christ shared with his compatriots the belief that God would fulfil the promise made through the prophets to establish his reign. He differed from them as to the nature of that reign and in his supreme confidence that God would bring it about. As Austin Farrer has written: 'Christ did not take the promises of God to be a jest, because they could not be literally fulfilled. He did not say 'In the face of roman power we can found no messianic kingdom here.' He said, 'In the face of roman power which excludes our messianic kingdom in the literal sense, we will see what sort of messianic kingdom God will make.' He kept the words and God changed the thing and so we still call him Christ, Messiah, King, but not in the pre-crucifixion sense. He kept the words; and when Caiaphas asked him: 'Art thou the Christ?' he said, 'I am.'; and when Pilate asked if he were the king of the Jews, he did not deny. But God changed the thing. The body of Jesus, first living, then dead, was trussed up and crucified as the Guy of literal messiahship, but God placed his true Messiah on the throne of heaven and in the hearts of his believers.'[5]

We need not suppose that Jesus saw clearly beforehand how the Father whom he wholeheartedly trusted would bring about his will. But he realised from the first that to commit himself to God's Kingdom meant challenging the forces of evil and facing their backlash. He expected his disciples too to share in that confrontation with the powers of darkness, and in the prayer he bequeathed to them three of its seven petitions are concerned with evil: evil in the past, evil in the future, evil in the present. Let us look at these petitions. The first is a prayer for forgiveness. 'Forgive us our trespasses as we forgive those who trespass against us.' The translation trespasses is unfortunate as it suggests a more deliberate transgression than the greek indicates. In St Luke the word translated trespasses, *hamartias*, means literally missing the mark, getting off target, while the greek word in St Matthew, also translated trespasses, is *opheilemata,* which means debts. The words used suggest that Jesus thought of sin much more as leaving undone things which ought to have been done than of conscious and deliberate wrongdoing. And this interpretation is reinforced by the teaching of some of the parables. In the parable of the talents the man with one talent is blamed not for stealing the talent but for leaving it unused. The foolish virgins were punished for forgetfulness. In the parable of the last judgment those on the king's left hand are sentenced for what they had failed to do. 'I was hungry and you gave me no meat; I was thirsty and you gave me no drink; I was naked and you did not clothe me; I was sick and in prison and you did not visit me.'[6] We cannot draw the conclusion that Jesus was indifferent to active wrongdoing, murder, robbery, adultery, false witness etc. Rather he thought of these positive sins as blatant instances of falling short. It would seem that Jesus is not prepared to draw a line between the falling short of the man who is trying to live a good life and that of the open wrong doer. All have missed the mark, all have left undone what they should have done. But if this judgment seems unexpectedly severe on 'good' people his teaching about forgiveness is unexpectedly gentle. The one condition of forgiveness is willingness to forgive others from the heart. It would seem that Jesus is less concerned to bring home to men their wickedness than their blindness and folly in ignoring God.

The second of the petitions about evil is the cryptic 'Lead us not into the time of trial.' It is a prayer to be spared the fearful time of troubles which it was believed would usher in the end of the world and the final establishment of God's reign. It should, I think, be understood as a prayer to be kept from unbearable temptation – the torturer's rack, for example. Jesus expects his disciples to live in the present, casting care about the future into the hands of God. But nightmare fears about the future can so haunt a person that he is incapable of giving himself to his present tasks. Coming events cast their shadows before them. The threat of destitution, of redundancy, of bereavement, of incurable illness, of disgrace, of imprisonment, of death, any of these is liable to shake a person's reliance on God; and so Jesus includes this petition about future evil in his prayer. Indeed he prayed it himself when in Gethsemane he said 'Father if it be possible let this cup pass from me.' This casting care about the future on God neither dispenses us from taking reasonable precautions against what is highly probable – it does not discourage insurance though it does over insurance; nor does it guarantee immunity from trouble. It is just the proper way for the believer to face future trial.

The third of these petitions about evil is the prayer 'Deliver us from evil.' Jesus sees his mission to proclaim and usher in the reign of God as including the deliberate assault upon the various forces of evil which were hindering that reign. Perhaps the most central of these resisting forces was human unbelief and mistrust. But this was itself part of an interwoven web of evil. A man's personal unbelief and mistrust is largely the effect of the unbelief and mistrust of the society that moulded his formative years and still influences him strongly. There is the dead weight of the past embodied in institutions, in laws and customs, in received opinions, which though not wholly bad fall far short of the principles of the Kingdom. Behind the all-pervading influence of social institutions there is the secret pressure of psychic evil, which modern psychiatrists usually describe in terms of mental illness, such as schizophrenia, or manic-depressive psychosis or obsessional neurosis, but which Jesus and his contemporaries understood as due to the intrusive influence of demons. Jesus attacked this web of evil by proclaiming the news of the coming reign of God, by healing the sick and by liberating the demon-possessed. And we cannot doubt that behind this active ministry of deliverance there was constant and confident prayer to the Father.

After the resurrection the disciples' hope of the Kingdom of God, which they had learnt from Jesus, underwent a change. The traumatic experience of Jesus's crucifixion followed by their surprise and joy at his return to them from the dead coloured their whole outlook. Christ, alive and present with them, himself the first fruits of the coming reign of God, takes the place of the Kingdom in their thought and preaching. St Paul the first great christian theologian, sees life in the Kingdom as life in Christ. Entry into the Church through Baptism is an identification with the dying and rising again of Christ. This identification is renewed through sharing in the Eucharist. He insists that the christian should live out this identification by a death to sin, that is letting go of old, selfish ways, and a rising with Christ, a laying hold of a new attitude to God and his fellows.[7] This idea of a symbolic dying may sound to some romantic, to others inhumanly ascetic. But death, understood as a letting go of the past in order to grasp the present and the future, is in complete harmony with life's fundamental laws.

Geoffrey Harding writes of physical death: 'We have been dying ever since our first beginning. When I look at you, everything I can see – skin, hair, fingernails, – is already dead and on its way out. To see something alive I should have to peer into the depths of your eyes. Life to be life, is continuously being renewed, and this involves continual dying. The proteins in the soft tissues of my finger, for instance, have to be renewed every hundred days, and so with the rest of me; every cell inside me is in a high state of flux, with a constant to-ing and fro-ing of tiny bits of me, all of which seem to know what they are up to (for no adequate reason that the physiologist can really claim to know). Nature made two enormous strides forward in the course of evolution; one was sex and the other was death. Between them they made possible the vast differentiation of living things and the fantastic variety of the forms which life takes. Death is necessary to life. It is probably true to say that what we think of as 'death', is the point at which we can no longer keep on dying fast enough to make further renewal possible. The process slows down and gets clogged up and comes to a halt.'[8] The physical death of the various cells of the body, which occur so that the whole body may be renewed, is paralleled by a similar process in an individual's personal growth. Satisfactory development demands a continual letting go of the past in order to confront the present and the future. An infant passes through many phases as he grows up into a child and later a man or woman. If he copes with the experiences and learns the lessons of each phase sufficiently he can pass on to the next phase free and uncluttered. He can say good-bye, he can die, to his past and go forward renewed to his future. It is part of our human condition that we cling to the past; we invest some of our psychic energy in past happenings painful and pleasant and so are to that extent deprived of the energy we need for facing the present and the future. The act of repression by which we push some painful memory out of consciousness and forget it is no exception to the tendency to cling to the past. For we do not get rid of a memory by repressing it; we merely make our grip on it the more difficult to loosen.

The experience of the past ought to illuminate the present and equip us for the future. Unfortunately the past can hold us in chains because we cannot let go of it. This clinging to the past is a prime evil from which we need deliverance. The believer through his identification with Christ finds himself able to let it go, to die to it, and so to press on in hope into the unknown future. It is particularly important to let go of old fears and old resentments. Though half forgotten they hold us back, they check and weaken our power of responding to God in the here and now. In the prayer 'Deliver us from evil' it is especially from mistrust and resentment that we seek to be freed and whatever forces may be keeping them alive.

## PRAYER AND THE TASKS OF LIFE

Jesus saw the forces of evil as a menace which today we are inclined to underestimate. But evil is often better resisted indirectly by strengthening our attachment to the good rather than by direct confrontation. And so, immediately preceding the three petitions concerned with evil, there is placed the prayer, 'Give us today our daily bread'. The petition asks for the strength needed to fulfil today's tasks; it affirms our day to day dependence on God's help. At each stage of life we are in need of strength to live life to the full, to learn the lessons and fulfil the tasks that belong to that stage, to let go of the seductive past and reach out to the bracing and exciting future. Petition for the particular strength I need opens me to receive from God what he wills to give but cannot unasked. Or perhaps the truth is stated better by saying that the firm reliance on God, which petition expresses and deepens, unbars the door to the grace which God desires to give, the door which mistrust and fear have held shut. People sometimes react against petition as expressing a servile attitude inappropriate to a human being, as a farm labourer might resent being expected to touch his cap to the squire. Such a reaction ignores our intimate and inescapable dependence on God, far greater than that of an infant on its mother. The God whom I address when I pray is a Presence, a Resource, a spiritual Energy, in the very centre of my being. To rely on God is a deeper, truer, more effective way of relying on myself than any self-reliance that excludes God. Petition made to the Wisdom who dwells within me enables me to cooperate with that Wisdom. God works in me so as to activate and inspire my own capacity for wisdom, so that my vision is no less truly my own for being God-inspired. The tendency to think of God anthropomorphically and of his influence as something extraneous and alien to us, like that of our fellow men, obscures the importance of petitionary prayer.

Petition becomes much more valuable and significant, I believe, if we bear in mind the teaching of the spiritual guides who affirm that God who is present everywhere is most surely to be found within. Petitionary prayer then becomes a powerful means not only of bringing a person and those surrounding him into harmony with God's will but also and equally of his self-realization.

In an earlier chapter I spoke of a kind of watershed in a person's life. Before the watershed our first task is to develop our humanity as far as possible, to grow to our full human stature; after it our task is to give ourselves away to God and to our neighbour. The task of developing our humanity in the first part of life is important, for the less I have been able to realize myself the less I shall have to give away and the less I shall be inclined to give it. In the first period a person must learn to grow out of the dependence of childhood into the responsibility of the adult, to launch himself on a career, to learn to do a job efficiently, or to begin to follow a vocation. Further he will need to form stable relationships of friendship and, in the majority of cases, to marry and with the help of his partner to make a home and care for a family. There is a minority called to a way of life which involves the renunciation of marriage in obedience to a call to serve the Kingdom in some way that rules out marriage and to love more widely than is possible for those bound closely to one person by the marriage bond. After the watershed a person needs to widen his concerns. It should be a period of growth in breadth of vision and in wisdom. But for this to take place a person must come to terms with the repressed and neglected bits of his own personality. For only those who possess themselves can give themselves away. People commonly learn to accept the neglected elements of their personality without any conscious decision to do so.

More often it comes about through yielding to a pressure from within. To fulfil the early tasks of life a person often has to renounce possibilities or interests which clash with his calling. The young barrister who is also a gifted musician will have for a time at least to give up his music in order to master his briefs; the girl who has done well at the Slade may have to renounce her art in order to get married, help make a home and raise a family. But later on these earlier interests return and seek recognition. Perhaps the barrister after taking silk is able to give more time to music and the wife and mother now that her children are in their teens sets up her easel again and resumes painting.

A man's prayers should change in order to keep pace with and foster his growth in humanity. Before the watershed his petition will tend to be for the faith, the courage, the practical skill and the generosity to respond to the changing needs and demands of people, of work and of society in general. He will seek for strength to cut his way through the jungle of difficulties and opportunities. After the divide his prayer will tend to circle round such ideas as surrender to God's will, becoming an instrument of the Kingdom, letting go and letting God have his way. The concerns of others will have an increasingly important place in his prayer. His horizon will be widening. He is beginning to see that life lost is life gained and that in the spiritual realm the only things you truly possess are the things you share.

To speak of a watershed or divide in a person's life is to suggest a much more definite turning point than is at all common. Sometimes indeed an important personal event does mark a decisive change in outlook, but far more often the transition is gradual and well nigh imperceptible, stretching over ten or fifteen years. Further those who are well into the second half of life are sometimes driven to complete the tasks that normally belong to early adulthood, adolescence or even childhood, but which for some reason were not adequately performed at the proper time. This could be caused by a childhood legacy of fear, resentment or self-rejection which, perhaps coupled with a discouraging environment, handicapped the person all through his early life. But it could also result from his seeking too early, following a mistaken ideal, to acquire the kind of relaxed self-awareness and passivity appropriate to the later years of life and leaving unfulfilled the tasks of youth. Through the twists and turns of his passage through life the believer can in prayer find an assured source of guidance and strength. He will discover this in proportion to his firm reliance on the God who is all the time addressing him through the people and circumstances that influence him but who is to be found most surely in the depths of his own being.

Jesus teaches the need to persevere in prayer. In order to drive home his point he startingly compares God to a lazy judge, who has to be badgered before he will try a case and see that justice is done, and to a man asleep at night, who has to be awakened and persuaded out of bed in order to lend three loaves to a neighbour.[9] Does Jesus imply by these parables that God is reluctant to answer prayer? His other teaching strongly affirms the opposite, that God is far more ready to hear than we to pray. The resistance that needs to be worn down by persistent prayer is not in God but in ourselves. There has grown up around us a wall of mistrust and scepticism. It is this barrier of unbelief that has to be battered down by repeated prayer. And the prayer that will in the end reduce the stoutest wall of doubt to rubble is the confident prayer of those who are sure of being heard, the prayer of commitment, the prayer of those wholeheartedly devoted to the reign of God.

The stress laid by Jesus on perseverance in prayer raises the practical question of how to resist the strong tendency to lose interest after a time and give up. It is to counter this tendency that many people find some kind of rule or method in prayer essential. A rule of prayer can ensure that we do not omit to pray through forgetfulness and the pressure of other interests and duties. A rule to give some time to prayer morning and evening focuses the general intention to pray on specific occasions, which can be planned and perhaps secured from interruption. At the same time rule is a means to an end and a rule of prayer is intended to foster the spirit of prayer. It is possible to make a rule a substitute for living in the spirit of prayer, which means to live under the guiding influence of the Holy Spirit, who cannot be organised or controlled. This possibility does not tell against having special times for prayer but only against giving undue importance to their precise observance. The late Dorothy Kerin has described how once she got up in the early morning, following strong intimation, to go to Holy Communion to pray for three friends of hers who were ill. During the service she had a kind of vision of Christ in the course of which she prayed earnestly for the three friends. Later in the day she learnt that they had become well. She had been guided by God to go to the place of prayer and to pray the prayer that he intended to answer. Whatever rule of method I follow it is important that I hold myself ready and open to the Holy Spirit, to listen for the inner voice or the gentle nudge that bids me pray the prayer that he can use as an instrument of healing or blessing. Method is good so long as it is the servant of inspiration and not a substitute for it.

All Jesus's teaching about prayer is about the prayer of petition. Thanksgiving was so much a part of Jewish religion that no doubt he took it for granted that his disciples would thank God as well as ask for his help. St Paul conjoins thanksgiving with petition; and I will conclude this chapter with some reflections on the prayer of gratitude, which is I believe of great spiritual importance. It is one of the ways we can escape the clutch of the past. When I thank God for past pleasure or happiness I make of the remembered enjoyment a springboard from which I leap into the caring arms of God. Thanksgiving detaches me from the past and anchors me in the present. It is not only an expression of gratitude, it is an affirmation of faith. Even the evils of the past, the fear, the guilt, the humiliation, the rejection experienced long ago but still alive in memory, can be matter for thanksgiving for those who believe that God is at work, healing the hurt, bringing good out of evil, liberating the good imprisoned by fear or chained to buried memories. I have referred earlier to the tendency to reject bits of ourselves because they do not fit in with a too narrow ideal. Thanksgiving can help to reverse this tendency and undo its ill effects. For to thank God who dwells in the depths of my being for the sex drive, for example, and the capacity to love and to fight is inevitably to make it more difficult to reject these dangerous gifts of God. It is well, I believe, to begin by thanking God for the ordinary blessings of life, for food when hungry, rest when tired, beautiful sights and sounds, friends, those who love us and those whom we love. By expressing gratitude for such things we earth our relationship with God in the simple satisfactions of daily life. We can go on to be grateful to God for spiritual blessings, for all that gives meaning to life, for the love of God disclosed in Jesus Christ, for his grace flowing through the fellowship and the sacraments of the Church. Finally we can thank God in trouble. It may be necessary before I can thank God from the heart to complain and protest, to give expression to my anger and despair. If these emotions are alive in me it is more honest as well as wiser to bring them out into the bright light of God's presence than to allow them to fester in the dark. 'Why do the wicked prosper? Why are the poor oppressed? Why have you forsaken me?' Only when, by putting them into words, we have got rid of some of the poison of bitterness and resentment shall we be able to turn to God in thanksgiving and praise. And this we do because we believe that God is at work, however hiddenly, bringing good out of evil and triumph out of tragedy. The supreme example of this and the surest guarantee of God's presence and power at work in the worst that we can imagine is the cross of Christ, in which blackest injustice is made the instrument of boundless blessing.

Thanksgiving can be an expression both of faith and of gratitude. It can but it need not; for it is possible to thank a person out of politeness without feeling grateful and to thank God out of a sense of duty with no feeling of gratitude. But when thanksgiving springs from a grateful heart it is the potent seed of love and trust. It is the natural response to the message of God's love made concrete in Jesus Christ once the truth has penetrated from the head into the heart. Sometimes the believer reflecting on the Love that made and redeemed him finds his heart suddenly on fire with a love which words altogether fail to express. He wants simply to look and love and exult in the presence of God, the Unknown who totally transcends his understanding. For, as *The Cloud of Unknowing* has it, 'By love may he be gotten and holden, but by thought never.'[10] But we have strayed here into the country of contemplation which is the subject of our next chapter.

1. Mk.11.24.
2. Jn. 14. 13, 15, 16.
3. Mk. 8. 35.
4. Mk. 14.36
5. *The Celebration of Faith* (Hodder & Stoughton, 1970) p. 34.
6. Matthew 25, 42, 43.
7. Rom. 6.34. Col. 2. 12 & 3.3.
8. New Fire. No. 15. (Summer 1973) p. 289.
9. Lk. 11.5–13 & 18. 1–8.
10. Chap. 6.

# 8. Looking and Loving

I said to my soul, be still, and let the dark come upon you
Which shall be the darkness of God.

T.S. Eliot, *East Coker* ll.112–113

## ATTENTIVENESS TO GOD

In chapter six I spoke of God's presence and of the importance
at the very outset of prayer of learning to focus the attention on
him. A normal preliminary to this is a reading and reflection
designed to rouse heart and mind to a consciousness of God.
Pictures whether mental or visible, images, words, phrases,
prayers, set or informal, all can serve as a help to awakening
the awareness of God. This attempt to realise the presence of
God is a preparation for any kind of prayer, private or
liturgical. In contemplation this realising God's presence,
waiting on him, listening to him, looking towards him,
becomes not just a beginning but the whole of prayer during
the time of meditation. The gratitude that issues in deeply felt
thanksgiving can lead a person to want just to rest in God's
presence in an attitude of trust, love, penitence, longing
dependence, now one of these attitudes predominating now
another. The saintly Curé D'Ars has told the story of the old
peasant, his parishioner, who used to kneel for an hour every
night with his eyes fixed on the tabernacle over the altar.
When asked by the Curé what he said during his nightly vigil
he replied: 'I don't say anything. I look at him and he looks at

me.' This kind of prayer is contemplation, which, if it were to be summed up in two words, might be called looking and loving. It is a looking towards God, a godward orientation of heart and mind, whence comes its name. It can also fittingly be called the prayer of the heart. More is meant by heart than just the seat of loving. The heart beats out of sight near the centre of the body. It stands also for the movements both of instinct and intuition that spring from our unknown depths. It is a region of our being not under reason's control. It has its own logic of which the sophisticated intelligence knows nothing. The prayer of the heart is a prayer involving us in depth.

A certain attentive passivity of mind is implied in the phrases 'waiting on God', 'listening to God', 'looking towards God'. Different kinds of people approach contemplation in different ways. For everyone contemplative prayer should involve so far as possible the focusing of the whole person, soul and body, heart and mind, in prayer. No effort of our own can bring this about for we are not in command of the whole of ourselves. Only God himself acting from the centre of our being can enable us to be wholly focused on him and only then with our cooperation. Contemplative prayer is a cooperating with the indwelling Spirit of God. How a person cooperates will depend on the kind of person he is, the quality of his intellect, the warmth of his heart, his upbringing and education and many other factors. I believe Jung's study of different human types can shed light on some of the ways in which a person may open himself to the leading of the Holy Spirit in prayer. The Swiss psychologist speaks of four ways in which men deal with life and its problems: through the senses – through seeing, hearing handling etc. – through thinking, through feeling and through intuition. He regards sensation and intuition as perceptive functions: through sensation we take note of the facts staring us in the face, through intuition of the possibilities suggested by the facts, the facts behind the facts. Thinking and feeling are judging functions: thinking judges things as true or false, feeling as good or bad. People vary according to which of these functions is strong or weak and on which they tend to rely most.

It would seem that the prayer of contemplation, of looking and loving, demands the cooperation especially of intuition and feeling. The importance of thinking and sensation is preparatory. Thinking is valuable as relating prayer to the world of people and events in which we live and can help to free us from superstition and credulity. Sensation, sight for example, can help by enabling us to attend to the signs and symbols that speak of God and so can enlist our depths in the turning to God. But intuition looks through the signs towards him to whom they point, while feeling which fastens on the good and rejects the bad enables a person to rest and delight in the presence of God. 'By love may he be gotten and holden but by thought never.' Contemplative prayer is usually focused initially on a picture, image, word or phrase which leads a person to drop reflection and just concentrate in love or trust or penitence on the image, word or idea. He looks through the image towards the Unknown to which it points. His attention naturally wavers from time to time, but he brings it back to his point of focus and can often remain thus for a long time without growing weary. It is a prayer of the heart because the concentration would be totally impossible if the heart, the depths, were not engaged. It is sometimes called the prayer of simplicity because it has a simple childlike quality about it. Many people pray in this way, their attention focused on a crucifix, for example, or a lighted candle, with the repetition of some phrase such as Light of the world or the Jesus prayer or a sentence from the psalms.

Those who pray thus may be drawn to a more intuitive type of contemplation, in which the senses, the imagination, the reasoning faculty become more completely subordinate to intuition. Jung has defined intuition as perception by way of the unconscious. The intuitive knows or believes he knows, for intuition is by no means infallible, without being able to say how he knows, he has hunches. A person knows 'unconsciously' far more than he is aware of. The unconscious is not only the repository of memory where all his past experiences are somehow recorded, but of all sorts of fleeting impressions picked up half-consciously, not attended to and promptly forgotten. It is in all probability the recipient of many kinds of telepathic messages from outside, only a tiny fraction of which come to the surface in a conscious idea or impression. The intuitive as it were listens to the unconscious and perhaps pays

attention to dreams or waking fantasies, which are the product
of unconscious thinking and feeling. He is like a man standing
on the shores of the great ocean of the unconscious waiting to
see what the waves will wash up onto the beach of consciousness. What he will perceive will depend on what his interests are. Those who are committed to God in their inten-
tions and actions will be led and fed by divine inspiration.
They will seize on the things they know are of God and neglect
the rest.

## INTUITIVE CONTEMPLATION

The procedure of someone who seeks God through the way of
intuition is markedly different from that of one who follows the
way of a more active concentration. For the former will try to
silence thinking in order to hold himself receptive to what God
may say or do within. Words or symbols may be used in either
approach to God but they will be used differently. In the one
case they will be used as focusing points of concentration, in
the other as means of keeping the active mind quiet and of
preventing it roaming around in a manner that might disturb
the inward waiting on God and listening to him. In active contemplation words are used as tools of thought, means to assist
concentration. In the more passive kind words are used as a
windscreen to protect the flame of prayer within, the godward
aspiration, from being blown out by distractions. The person
praying thus knows what the words he uses mean but he does
not think what they mean. Concentrated thinking seems to interfere with the movement of trust and longing that rises up
from the depths. One of the sayings of the first Christian
monks is 'Short prayer pierces heaven'. One reason for this is
that brief ejaculations don't involve reflection and so can
enable the heart to speak simply and directly without interference from the head. Similarly the author of *The Cloud of
Unknowing* recommends the use of a little word, preferably a
monosyllable, such as God or Love.

I have written as though a person can choose whether he
will follow the way of more active contemplation or the more

intuitive way, the way of unknowing. But which way he
follows lies largely outside his choice. He must follow as he is
led. In the spiritual journey there are two kinds of growth
which the Spirit fosters in those who respond to him: growth
in the awareness of God, which is in part psychological, and
growth in a loving committedness to God in heart and will and
action which overflows in the love of other people. The second
of these is immeasurably the more important; the other is one
of the helps – and a powerful one – to growth in this loving
commitment. How much a person may become conscious of
God's presence depends partly on God's invitation and his
response to it, partly on temperament, itself God's gift, and
partly on training.

I pointed out earlier that contemplation on its human side is
a response to God through intuition; and intuition can be
trained. In other words perception through listening to the unconscious can be strengthened by systematic exercise. This is
precisely what many of the schools of meditation which have
grown up in this country during the past fifteen years set out to
do. There are various ways of training intuition, but the
schools of meditation seem all to have this feature in common.
They all employ some mental device which silences or reduces
active, controlled thinking. The method of doing this in
Transcendental Meditation is to repeat one of the names of
God in Sanskrit. The rhythm, the monotony, ignorance of the
meaning of the words lulls the active, reasoning mind into
quiescence and so enables intuition to work. The method of
zen meditation is quite different. It encourages a relaxed
posture but silences the reasoning mind by means of the koan,
which is an insoluble riddle that defeats reason. For example
one famous koan asks the question 'What is the sound of one
hand clapping?' Reason in the end gives up and intuition
comes into play. Another help to quietening restless reason is
attention to the breathing, noticing the breath entering and
leaving the lungs, or to the heart beat. Another way of awakening intuition is through concentration on some visible object, a
flower, say, or a lighted candle. The eastern mandala, a circle
or square, sometimes intricately patterned, having a centre, is
just such a visible symbol designed to evoke intuition. The
crucifix has been used for centuries in this way, To arouse in-

tuition it is important not to *think* about the meaning of the
symbol but to let it speak to you. It is the same with the
repetition of a prayer formula, such as the Jesus prayer; if contemplative intuition is to be evoked, then the words must be
allowed to communicate their meaning without deliberate
reflection on them.

The growth of schools of meditation of largely oriental inspiration has been disconcerting to many Christian teachers of
prayer following their own mystical tradition. Even more disconcerting has been the interest of scientists including some
medical men. It was discovered some fifty years ago that the
brain gives off minute electrical impulses which can be
measured.[1] The electro-encephalograph registers various types
of consciousness by means of different and easily recognizable
waves in a graph. When thinking actively a person's brain
registers beta waves. When he shuts his eyes and turns his
attention inwards usually the beta waves stop and alpha waves
are registered; and in deep meditation or contemplation high
amplitude alpha waves are drawn on the register. It seems that
those who are proficient in Transcendental Meditation, Zen or
Christian contemplation all register high amplitude alpha
waves on the encephalograph. Doctors are interested in this
because the state is thought to be beneficial to health. The
breathing becomes slower and quieter, the heart beat slows,
the blood pressure drops. On the other hand meditation of this
intuitive kind need not be religious at all. There are those who
meditate twice a day and claim not to believe in anything. The
object of their meditation is to improve their health and
develop their human potential. It may even have the quite
specific end of making them more effective business executives
or motor salesmen. The fact that meditation can be a means to
wholly secular ends is a salutary reminder not to over-rate the
ability to enter into a state of deep intuitive concentration. The
object of the exercise is all-important, not the exercise in itself.
The fact that this kind of meditation can be used as a means to
quite different ends is no reason for neglecting a way that has
helped many Christians to grow in love for God and their
neighbour. Similar physical concomitants can accompany
very diverse experiences. A person may feel sick with anxiety,
sick with grief and sick with joy. The same feeling of nausea

can have different, indeed opposite meanings.

This new understanding of the physiological basis of mental activity during prayer need not in any way alter our estimate of prayer. Rather it should set us free from any tendency to judge its validity by the degree of concentration attained. St Teresa, the great sixteenth century spanish teacher of interior prayer, who is deeply interested in psychological states during prayer and classifies prayer according to the extent to which a person is wholly concentrated in it, affirms that the only sure test of its value or indeed of its genuineness is its fruit in daily life. For the loving commitment to God which is expressed in prayer must if genuine issue in a growing commitment in daily life.

The French spiritual writer, Father Poulain,[2] regards what he calls the ligature as a distinguishing mark of the more passive contemplation. The word, ligature, refers to a kind of binding or inhibiting of the power of controlled thinking during prayer, so that a person is unable to concentrate on the idea of God or Christ while praying; to do so he must stop praying. St John of the Cross gives the inability to meditate (in the sense of controlled thinking) during prayer as one of the signs that a person should stop trying to think about spiritual realities during prayer and follow the way of intuition or un-knowing, in which thinking is deliberately discarded. There is confirmation of the reality of the ligature from the encephalograph which discloses that the brain waves registered during passive contemplation are of a different kind from those registered in controlled thinking and that normally it is impossible – or only after prolonged practice – to register both types of brain wave, that is both alpha and beta, simultaneously.

I have referred to St John of the Cross, the younger contemporary of St Teresa, and like her a great teacher of contemplation. There are interesting parallels to his teaching about the spiritual journey in the writings of Roberto Assagioli,[3] the twentieth century psychologist. His system of psychological training, called psychosynthesis, consists of two parts or stages, that of personal and that of spiritual psychosynthesis. The first stage is designed to help the individual to develop the qualities of a complete and responsible citizen.

The system aims at helping him to learn to face and manage the instinctive drives within him and to respond to the needs and claims of others: in a word to develop the kind of strength of character which Erikson terms ego strength. Many people never go beyond this stage. Others are drawn perhaps in middle life, perhaps earlier, to the second stage which it is the aim of spiritual psychosynthesis to foster. It is the teaching about spiritual psychosynthesis that is reminiscent of the spanish friar. One of the striking features of psychosynthesis is Assagioli's conviction that the human personality is grounded in what he variously calls 'the higher centre', 'the higher self', 'the transcendent self', but which I shall call simply the centre. The 'lower' centre, with which Assagioli contrasts the 'higher' centre corresponds roughly to the ego, the conscious directing personality. In the second stage of psychosynthesis the higher centre, or the centre as I call it, becomes the focus of development. The bridge between these two stages of the spiritual journey is called by Assagioli the awakening. The awakening is caused by an awareness of the centre which breaks into a person's consciousness and by its magnetic attraction. This awareness according to Assagioli is both preceded and followed by a crisis. The crisis which precedes and prepares for the awakening is a feeling of emptiness, a sense of the unreality of things which previously had seemed important, a feeling that life had become meaningless. It is caused by the withdrawal of psychic energy from the sphere of the ego, the sphere of planning and thinking about life's practicalities, to the centre.

This is strikingly reminiscent of the teaching of St John of the Cross.[4] The manner and tone of the spanish friar is very different from that of the italian psychologist. The latter aims at the cold objectivity of scientific description, the former writes as one passionately committed to the journey. The one gives a bare map of the road, the other a traveller's description of it. St John of the Cross interprets the experience in the light of the christian faith as understood by a trained theologian. He does not speak of the centre but of God, though he does speak of God as dwelling in the soul's centre. He likens the journey to a mountain ascent in the pitch blackness of a moonless night. The journey is a movement of aspiration towards an Unknown that is infinitely precious. The metaphor of darkness points to at least three realities.[5] First there is the loss of the daylight of the old way of thinking about God; ideas and doctrines which have nourished a person's spiritual life lose all savour, they are not so much disbelieved as felt to be unreal. This is a painful trial to those whose faith has meant much to them. Secondly the night is a darkness caused by faith itself, operating in an unfamiliar mode; it is faith, not as belief in certain propositions, nor even as belief in the reality to which the propositions point, but as an intuition reaching out blindly to a Reality which draws it but which totally transcends its grasp. Thirdly the dark night speaks of God himself, the Unknown, the Transcendent, whose light dazzles us and whose ways are beyond our understanding. A gradual reversal of values takes place in the journeying soul for whom old landmarks have disappeared, who has to learn to disregard what it knows and love what it does not know. Everything has to be judged by one sole criterion: whether it helps or hinders growth into conformity with the One who dwells in the centre of his being. The only light to guide the steps of the spiritual mountaineer is a light burning in his heart. The same light of loving aspiration towards God occupies the central place in the teaching of the english fourteenth century *Cloud of Unknowing*. Like the dark night the cloud of unknowing is a symbol both of the transcendent God who cannot be grasped by the reasoning intelligence and of the blind, trusting intuition that reaches out towards him. 'Strike the thick cloud of unknowing with a sharp dart of longing love and on no account think of giving up.'[6] And again 'this little blind loving of God beating away at this cloud of unknowing all else buried away.'[7] The darkness of contemplation which these two writers describe is a darkness or blankness of the conscious mind which feels its ignorance and incapacity. It is, as we have seen, due to an intuitive awareness of God, who is obscurely known by certain effects within, a mysterious inner urge and orientation, a yearning of love towards an unknown presence. The attraction towards the centre of which Assagioli writes is in fact, I believe, an attraction towards God who addresses the soul through the centre.

Before going on to speak further of Assagioli's teaching I

wish to illustrate the fact that Christian contemplation is not just a thing of the distant past, and I will give a further description of contemplative prayer, this time from a twentieth century teacher of prayer, the late Dom John Chapman, Abbot of Downside some forty years ago. In matter of fact tones he writes. 'This time of prayer is passed in the act of wanting God. It is an idiotic state and feels like the completest waste of time until it gradually becomes more vivid. The strangest phenomenon is when we begin to wonder whether we mean anything at all, and whether we are addressing anyone, or merely repeating mechanically a formula we do not mean. The word, God, seems to mean nothing. If we feel this curious and paradoxical condition we are starting on the right road, and we must beware of trying to think what God is and what he has done for us etc, because this takes us out of prayer and spoils God's work, as St John of the Cross says.'[8] The prayer that the abbot describes is the same prayer of the heart, in which the head's share is thoroughly subordinate, that the two older authors describe. It is deliberate thinking that stops this intuitive contemplation. Thoughts may well go on automatically as a background to contemplation without our willing it. All we can do is to ignore them as far as possible, perhaps with the help of some verbal formula as suggested earlier. The abbot insisted that the person who in prayer renounced all deliberate thinking must think about the things of God when not praying. He needs to consecrate not only his intuition but his reason, imagination and common sense. These other faculties may be enlisted through reading, writing or speaking which brings them into play as well as by practical action in the service of other people.

## PROBLEMS, DANGERS AND REWARDS OF CONTEMPLATION

Assagioli speaks of two crises, one before and one after the awakening to the pull of the centre. The first crisis is the one we have just considered, the loss of interest and meaning of the ideas, ideals and activities which had earlier seemed important. The second crisis is caused by the invasion of the conscious mind by vivid spiritual insights and impressions, by a feeling of expansion and new energy. The person who experiences this for the first time is apt to be elated by this spiritual illumination and tends to lose his objectivity and sense of proportion. He tends to think of this light and energy as his own possession and to become somewhat inflated. What is happening is that a shift of the seat of control within the personality is beginning. Before the awakening the consciously held ideas and ideals of a person tend to suppress or repress desires and impulses that conflict with them. But with the withdrawal of psychic energy away from the old conscious aims and ideas towards the centre the repressing force is weakened, with the consequence that the desires and impulses long kept under stream up into consciousness in the form of violent new temptations or the recrudescence of old ones. A person may find himself plagued with blasphemous or doubting thoughts, with feelings of rage, hate or depression, with crude sex temptations or with dark suspicions about his friends. The contrast between the sense of new spiritual insight and energy and these other unwanted impulses and desires, which are probably a relic of childhood frustrations, apparently grown out of but living an underground existence and ready to make their presence felt if there is any weakening of the restraining pressure, can be both confusing and discouraging to the spiritual traveller. In time, all being well, these energies will be brought under the control of the centre and will form a valuable element in a transmuted personality. But during the transition period which may last a long time, perhaps for years rather than months, the individual will undergo much stress and strain. He is liable to get discouraged and is tempted to give up only to find that he cannot return to his condition before the awakening.

The practice which Assagioli recommends as enabling a person to manage these invasions from the unconscious he calls by the formidable name of disidentification. He states the principle underlying the practice of disidentification as follows: 'We are dominated by everything with which our self becomes identified. We can dominate and control everything from which we disidentify ourselves.'[9] There is an ambiguity contained in the word dominate. A man may be said to dominate the desires and impulses that surge up from within him in the sense that a canoeist may be said to dominate the swift-flowing river on which he paddles his canoe and is not carried away or capsized by the current. We don't dominate our unconscious in the sense of not being all the time dependent on it. The principle of disidentification is of the utmost importance and we meet it under different names in the writing of the spiritual guides. One name for it is detachment which is remarkably similar to Assagioli's attitude of the observer. 'I am aware of my desires, my feelings, my thoughts, my inspirations, but I am other than these; I am their judge and master; I am responsible for the way I use them.' This attitude of the detached observer needs to be balanced by the realisation of dependence on the desires and inspirations that I observe in myself, just as the canoeist knows the dependence of his canoe on the river that bears it. The attitude of detachment without any realisation of dependence is typical of the schizoid personality. The word dominate suggests the battle that a person must be prepared to fight if he is to keep his canoe on course, if he is not to be swept away by the powerful energies of the unconscious. To be able to do this successfully the ego needs to have attained a certain strength. It is particularly important for a person to avoid being deceived into identifying with the spiritual urges and intuitions that come into his mind. These should be regarded as things which happen to him, perhaps as gifts which he has the task of using responsibly, perhaps as movements of the mind to be looked at critically and not to be assumed without question to be either true or significant. A person needs to cultivate something of John Keats' negative capability: 'When a man is capable of being in uncertainties, mysteries, doubts, without any irritable reaching after fact and reason.' A person needs to cultivate an awareness of the impulses from within without either repressing them or acting them out. He has to learn to tolerate them with patience and without anxiety until gradually the centre takes control.

There are certain risks about the way of unknowing if it is undertaken before a person is ready and inwardly equipped for it. I mention two dangers in particular. The first is that of discouragement which may lead to the abandonment of the whole spiritual journey. The looking inwards, waiting on what may emerge from the depths may expose a person to dark energies which he has neither the strength nor the skill to manage. He may become acutely anxious or depressed and feel that he is going to the bad, partly from the ignorance of in-experience, partly because he is unable to manage the uprush of what seems overwhelming temptation.

The second danger is that of mistaking a false con-templation for the genuine thing. The encephalograph has shown that the inner activity of transcendental meditation, zen meditation  and christian contemplation are accompanied by precisely similar electrical impulses in the brain, which are very different from those occurring during concentrated thinking. Further these meditative and contemplative states of mind are commonly found to have a tranquillizing influence on the individual and to be beneficial to health. It would seem possible to induce, either deliberately by means of special techniques, or by accident, this kind of brain activity with its helpful side-effects without any real commitment to God in love and trust. I might argue that this might not be a bad thing even if it is not genuine contemplation. Well, but to indulge in this mental activity believing it to be true prayer is to deceive myself, which is surely bad. Further, to persist in this quietist activity believing it to be prayer would, I do not doubt, tend to make me self-satisfied and to render me insensitive to the needs and claims of others and my responsibilities in the world. The teachers of prayer are well aware of the danger of this kind of self-deception. The surest test they give of the genuineness of prayer is the fruits it bears in daily life. 'By their fruits you shall know them.'

The old spiritual guides, well aware of both these dangers, insist on the importance for one setting out on the way of con-templation or intuitive prayer to consult and seek the guidance of some more experienced traveller. The great number of books that are today available may to some extent reduce the importance of the personal guide. But books can never wholly take the place of a wise director. A book cannot give the reassurance, the encouragement and sometimes the straight warning that may be what I need. Again it is possible for me to misread books and to suppose mistakenly that my experience in prayer is the same as that described, just as a person browsing through a medical dictionary may mistakenly imagine he suffers from some of the diseases there encountered. Further it is not easy to be sure in our own case about the fruits of prayer in our daily life. For one thing fruit does not ripen in a day. It takes time for the inward change brought about through the growing orientation towards God to express itself in action; it has to overcome the resistance of long-standing habit as well as of the unchanged expectations of others. It is clearly of great value to be able to turn for advice to some wise and experienced spiritual guide. Unfortunately such guides are few, and always have been, and are not easy to find. Some are discovering a helpful alternative through membership in a small intimate group whose members share spiritual experiences and spiritual problems. Such a group may be able to give both the encouragement and reassurance that the individual needs as well as the common sense and realism to correct possible self-deception.

But if there are dangers in wait for those who tread the way of unknowing, there are also great rewards. For as a person learns more and more to commit himself in trust to the Unknown who dwells in the centre of his being he finds himself growing in freedom and peace. This growth is uneven for it involves facing one by one the unfinished tasks of earlier life and elements of himself which had been repressed. As each of these missed opportunities and buried bits of himself comes up into consciousness it is felt first as a threat to what he has now become, then as a problem he can live with and finally as an enrichment and enlargement of his personality. Some of the repressed elements are the relics of forgotten childish ways, grown out of but obscurely alive: childish jealousy, childish greed, childish self-centredness. As he acknowledges and owns these childish impulses and attitudes they change. They impart to him increasingly a child-like character: child-like simplicity, child-like spontaneity, child-like openness. He experiences the paradoxical sense of belonging increasingly to God and to other people and at the same time of being himself, of being his own man as never before.

The life of commitment in love and trust to God and to

others is the true goal not simply of contemplative prayer, not only of the christian life, but, so the christian believes, of all human life; contemplative prayer is just a powerful means of attaining it. But the christian life cannot be rightly understood as the life of an individual on his own, it is a life lived in interdependence with his fellow believers. And this essential corporate dimension of Christian living expresses itself in corporate prayer and worship which will be the subject of the next chapter.

1. There is an interesting account of the different kinds of brain wave in *Silent Music* by William Johnston (Collins, 1974). Chapter 3, Brainwave and Biofeedback.
2. *The Graces of Interior Prayer* (Kegan Paul, Trench, Trubner & Co.)
3. Op. cit.
4. *Ascent of Mount Carmel*
5. Op. cit. Bk. 1. Ch.2.
6. The Cloud. Ch.6.
7. Op. cit. Ch.12.
8. *The Spiritual Letters of Don John Chapman O.S.B.*, (Sheed & Ward, 1935) p. 290.
9. Assagioli op. cit. p. 22.

# 9. The Pilgrim People

> the communication
> Of the dead is tongued with fire beyond the language of the living.
> T.S. Eliot, *Little Gidding* ll. 50–51.

The need for corporate worship springs partly out of man's social nature. God makes himself known to us in the first place through other people. We need others to awaken our capacity to recognise and acknowledge him. The infant becomes aware of God all unknowingly through his parents, especially his mother. He does not of course know what the word, God, means, but he is surrounded by a presence, a care, a warmth, a protection, a resource in trouble which, though mediated through his mother is ultimately from God. When later he learns about God and his care for all his creatures he will understand this as of a piece with the love he received from his parents. A person who never in childhood had the experience of being loved has difficulty in realising and responding to God's love. This dependence upon others for our awareness of God, though it diminishes as we grow older, never disappears. The faith and love of his fellow believers is a necessary support to the individual christian.

This was taken for granted by the first christians. The gospel summoned men to repent and be baptised, that is to change the direction of their lives and to be reborn into the community of believers. Today a christian will tend to think of himself as one who holds certain beliefs and adheres to certain ethical standards. He does not usually in the first place think of himself as the committed member of a community, sharing the community's faith and meeting God through its fellowship. But this was the unquestioned assumption of the first christians. To them it would have seemed incomprehensible that a person should wish to be a christian and at the same time stand aloof from the christian community. What would have been the point of claiming the christian name and then, by isolating yourself from the believing community, refusing the new life and freedom which God gave through membership in it? An individualism that excludes the sense of our spiritual dependence on others blinds a person to part of the gospel.

## WORSHIP AS SACRAMENTAL

Christian corporate worship should be in the broadest sense sacramental; that is to say it should make the fullest use of outward and visible signs to enable people in their innermost depths to share in and respond to the spiritual realities to which the signs point. I have earlier referred to the importance of symbols for the individual praying alone in order to involve the whole person, his emotions and his irrational depths in his approach to God. But what is important for the individual in private becomes essential for men and women praying together. For signs, visible and audible, are necessary to unite all together in worship, to focus their attention simultaneously on what is being done. A sacrament is a powerful sign which both expresses a spiritual meaning and brings about an inner change in those who are ready to be changed. The unseen Creator makes himself known through things which can be seen and heard, touched and smelt, tasted and eaten. In this way he addresses the whole of us, heart and mind, body and soul together. Further he addresses individuals as members one of another and in and through this mutual membership.

A sacrament is meant to be a living symbol in the sense of a powerful sign, focusing the imagination, releasing the emotions, moving to action. Unfortunately symbols can go dead, they can lose their power to speak to our depths; they degenerate into mere signs which express in a kind of shorthand what could be put more fully and accurately in words. The dead symbol can be restated in propositions which the mind can grasp, but it cannot move us. Corporate worship should use every means to bring the old symbols to life, to enhance their power to grip the imagination, stir our depths and rouse us to action. In practice public worship has been intellectualized, it has been made too much a matter of words and intellectual concepts; there is too little to appeal to the senses and to the imagination; the body is not enough involved as it needs to be if worship is to fulfil its function.

This is not the place nor have I the qualifications to describe the work of contemporary liturgists and pastors who are trying to revivify corporate worship. But I will illustrate what I believe is the direction which change should take by mentioning some of the ways in which, whether in informal groups or in church services people are learning to express their worship in symbolic acts, acts which express a meaning which could not be put into words. The kiss of peace, whether an embrace or a handshake, signifies the union and fellowship of the worshippers. Lifting up the arms expresses a certain openness to God and also the spirit of praise. Walking in procession symbolizes the Church as a pilgrim body on the move. Dancing expresses the spirit of joyful celebration. The act of corporate prostration signifies the spirit of worship and adoration. There are certain traditional gestures of the priest in the celebration of the Eucharist; in some groups the worshippers as far as possible make the same gestures, signifying that the whole congregation is celebrating the Eucharist with the officiating priest. These are put forward as hints and suggestions as to the direction of possible change. The renewal of worship must be worked out in practice by experiment. Time is needed for people to learn new ways of worship nor is every experiment likely to be successful. But I believe that the more the body can participate in worship by symbolic acts, the more worshippers will be led into a conscious realisation of the presence of God.

The supreme example of the sacramental principle is the Incarnation, in which the Word was made flesh, in which the unseen Creator took the visible creation to himself by becoming man, in which matter was intimately conjoined with eternal Spirit. Jesus Christ himself is the first and chief sacrament. The Dutch theologian, Edward Schillebeeckx,[1] has called Christ the sacrament of our encounter with God. His manhood, indeed his whole life, death and resurrection, is the powerful sign of our meeting with God. Through Christ our Maker grasps us, makes himself known to us, remakes us. But this cannot happen automatically; we have to recognize him and respond to him with a faith which includes both trust and commitment. When he walked the earth of Palestine most people, despite his teaching and his works of healing and deliverance failed to recognize him for what he was and so were excluded from the gifts he came to bring. Only those who recognised him and committed themselves to him found him to be indeed their way into a new relationship to God, to be in truth the powerful sign of their encounter with the living God.

Father Schillebeeckx goes on to affirm that the Church is the sacrament of Christ, the sign of his presence, a means of his action. This is an arresting interpretation of St Paul's image of the Church as the Body of Christ. St Paul speaks of christians as 'in Christ', an idea which may have sprung from the experience of Christ's presence in the groups of christians gathered for worship. St Paul understood each group of christians in the various cities he visited as somehow incarnating in its own place the whole Church of God with Christ as its head. The christians at Corinth and Ephesus are the Church of God which is at Corinth and the Church of God which is in Ephesus.

I believe nothing is more important for the rejuvenation of corporate worship than the recovery of an understanding of the sacramental character of the Church, of the perception of it as the powerful sign of Christ's presence. To approach worship without any understanding of Christ's presence in the Church would be precisely similar to sharing in the eucharistic liturgy and receiving communion without any understanding of Christ's presence there. A person participating in the Eucharist in a purely formal way without any perception of its spiritual meaning would be unlikely to profit much from his being in church and he might even have his spiritual sensibility blunted by his ignorance and imperceptiveness. I believe that a principal reason for the distaste which many modern christians feel for Church worship is their failure to perceive its sacramental significance.

What needs to be remedied is not just an ignorance that could be corrected by a simple course of instruction. The problem is one of a spiritual blindness, an unawareness, which can only be removed if the heart can be quickened. The truth that can renew our understanding of worship is a truth that can only be conveyed by symbols. For symbols not only rouse the heart, they enable us to grasp fact; indeed it is because we find contact with complex reality through them that they are able to speak powerfully to the heart. Austin Farrer has written: 'there is a current and exceedingly stupid doctrine that symbol evokes emotion and exact prose states reality. Nothing could be further from the truth; exact prose abstracts from reality, symbol presents it. And for that reason symbols have something of the many-sidedness of wild nature.'[2] There is of course a need for exact prose statement. Symbols are so rich in meaning, as wild nature is often so profuse and tangled, that there needs to be a paring down, an exclusion of false meanings. But before this task of path-making through the jungle of meanings that symbols suggest can usefully proceed, we need to amplify the meaning of the symbols, to allow them to speak to us, to call up images and ideas associated with them. Only then should we attempt to whittle them down into precise statements and useful but limiting concepts.

## THE PEOPLE OF GOD

I propose in this chapter to speak of worship in the context of three symbols, three powerful images of the Church. The first of these is the people of God, the new Israel. This symbol is especially appropriate today when we have learnt to think inclusively of christians belonging to other denominations than our own, when we think of them as brothers separated from us rather than as strangers or rivals. For the people of God easily accommodates the idea of differently organised bodies and communities gathered within its unity. But from the beginning, long before our modern divisions, it was a powerful symbol of the Church. The first christians, most of them Jews, saw themselves as the true heirs of the old Israel that had given them birth. In particular they saw Israel in its wanderings in the wilderness as the eloquent sign of their own discipleship. Israel after its miraculous deliverance from slavery in Egypt and its equally miraculous escape from Pharaoh's pursuing army by the passage of the Red Sea, was miraculously supplied with food and drink in the desert and led to Mount Sinai, where they received the ten commandments at the hands of Moses. Finally they were led into the promised land by a leader who bore the same name as Jesus the Messiah. The first christians took to themselves this ancient story. They had been delivered out of a moral and spiritual slavery resembling that of Egypt; Christ's death on the cross was a new Passover sacrifice, the triumphant crossing of the Red Sea outpouring of the Spirit at Pentecost was a new Sinai, the giving not of commandments inscribed on stone but of a law written in the heart, a new personal but shared knowledge of God.

These are some of the parallels by which the first christians amplified for themselves this powerful symbol of the Church. I believe that if our worship is to seem meaningful and relevant today we must let this and other symbols of the Church speak to our imaginations and hearts. This world is not our permanent home, we are strangers and pilgrims, looking for a promised land beyond this world; and yet the eternal life of the country we seek is not wholly in the future but something we are beginning to enjoy now. We journey not through space but through time. We walk by faith in One whom we cannot see. The worship of the Church is part of the corporate affirmation of faith by which the pilgrim people meet to encourage one another and to recall the ground of their faith and the goal of their journey. The journey is a movement of growth into fuller union with God, into a kind of knowing or experience of God. This experience cannot be adequately conceptualized, it cannot be stated in simple statements of fact. Symbol and poetry convey a better idea of it than any statements in prose. But it transcends man's powers of description. At the same

time it has to be expressed however imperfectly, partly to
strengthen the understanding's grasp of a reality only obscurely known, partly that it may be shared. Doctrine and dogma
are an attempt to express in words some outline of the experience of faith. Their principal function is to point to the
Unknown whom we worship and indicate the direction in
which he is to be found. Their secondary function is the
negative one of blocking the way to false paths.

Part of the worship of the pilgrim Church may be the recitation of a summary of its beliefs in the creed. This is best understood as an act of praise, as a rehearsing in briefest outline of
what the Lord has done for his people and what he has declared
himself to be. But the precise statements of the creed are not
the typical expressions of the faith and hope of pilgrims. These
are better declared in hymn and psalm, in song and carol, in
procession and dance which can give stronger and sweeter
voice to the spirit of praise and rejoicing than any bare
statement of belief. Christians as together they travel towards
their goal should be like men marching towards the dawn their
faces lit with the rays of the rising sun:

'Through the night of doubt and sorrow
Onward goes the pilgrim band,
Singing songs of exultation,
Marching to the promised land.'

One particular doctrine, that of the Holy Trinity, is so important for christian faith and so colours christian worship
that it demands specific mention. This doctrine of the Triune
God safeguards the primitive experience of redemption, which
is threefold. It sprang out of faith in the one true and living
God of the Old Testament Scriptures, the Creator, the ultimate Source of all that is. It involved total commitment to
Christ, who in his life on earth lived in a unique intimacy with
God, as an only Son with a Father, to Christ who taught,
healed the sick and delivered men from the power of demons,
who was put to death unjustly and on the third day was raised
from the dead to become the invisible but ever present leader
of the people of God. Finally it was the experience of and
reliance upon a new power and energy working in them, the

power of Jesus, guiding, renewing and uniting them, but a power distinguishable from Jesus as the Holy Spirit. The christian faith in God was a single, unitary faith in the one living God, but it was experienced in this triple mode. The doctrine of the Holy Trinity is the attempt to formulate the experience in words which will safeguard it and prevent it from being explained away. But once formulated it points to what could not have been foreseen: the conception of God not as bare, lonely unity but as society overflowingly rich; the conception that in him there is an eternal giving and receiving, a surrender and acceptance, a letting go and taking hold; that he not only loves but in his essential being is Love. To be on the Godward journey with the pilgrim people is to be taken more and more completely into the giving and receiving of the Godhead, to be initiated into and to become more and more at home in relationships of love.

Part of the worship of the people of God is a listening. In an earlier chapter I spoke of contemplative prayer as a kind of listening. There can be a corporate, silent listening to God's Word, spoken so deep within that only the attentive ear can recognise his voice. There is also a listening to the inward voice of God during the reciting of the psalms in monastic prayer. The rhythmical recitation of the familiar words lulls the active mind and disposes the monk to listen to the Word spoken within. But there is another kind of listening to the Word, through the spoken words of men. There is the reading aloud of Holy Scripture, the telling and retelling of the story of redemption, the story of man's creation, of his failure to respond to his creator and his consequent estrangement from him and from his own destiny, of the saga of the patriarchs and the rest of the sacred history leading up to the climax of the Scriptures, the story of the mighty deeds of the Redeemer.

An important part of worship is the listening to God's Word spoken through what St Paul calls the folly of preaching. He calls preaching folly because it proclaims truths about God and his self-disclosure in Christ which go far beyond the sober expectations of common sense and are not susceptible of proof. The words of the preacher must carry conviction by their power to illuminate the hearts of men and the things of God and to awaken faith. There are other functions of preaching.

The preacher has to point out the richness and depth of the symbols in which the faith is presented and to point out how they illuminate the contemporary world. For to do their work effectively symbols have to be related not only to man's inner world but to the world of every day, to the practicalities of getting a living and acting responsibly as a member of society. The preacher needs, like St Paul, to relate the duties of husband and wife, of parents and children, of employer and employed, to the powerful images of faith, to the self-giving of Christ and the renewing energy of the Spirit. Without the sense of the power and relevance of the Christian symbols and the realities to which they point preaching is likely to degenerate into dull moralising and prosy platitudes. There is further a prophetic function in preaching, the task of declaring God's presence and purpose in present day society, national and international, of making evident in contemporary events the action of God in mercy and judgment. Through the words of preachers of widely varying gifts and abilities God speaks to the minds and hearts of men. We lose immeasurably by failing to see the sacramental function of preaching. God speaks through human words; and blindness to his power at work in the sometimes trite and jejune words of men is likely to prevent that meeting with God which is one of the objects of the sermon. No doubt the spiritual imperceptiveness or the sloth or arrogance of the preacher may equally make difficult the confrontation with God that the sermon is meant to assist. But the preacher is greatly helped in discharging his formidable task by the attitude of a congregation which listens expecting to hear the Word of God sounding through his words.

One of the temptations of the children of Israel in the wilderness was to idolatry. The People of God today are equally tempted to the worship of false gods. It has been said that there are no atheists: a man's god is the thing he values most. This might equally be said of societies. A society's gods are the objects to which it gives supreme value. Such false gods are usually aims or values good in themselves but given supreme or at least exaggerated importance. Materialism, nationalism, humanitarianism are each of them an undue valuation of something good. The worship of the one true God is the surest protection against this kind of idolatry. One of the means by which the people of God is helped to detach itself from contemporary idolatry is through the preaching of the Word, another is the liturgy. The liturgy, which continually renewed and brought up to date, as it must be, comes from the past and is redolent of the past, is a  powerful corrective of the exaggerated and one-sided influence of contemporary ideas. Every age has its special insights, whose importance it tends to exaggerate, and its blindnesses, which it is unaware of. It is important that the special insights of a new generation should find expression in worship. But the conservative structure of the liturgy can prevent the half-forgotten truths of the past from being swamped and relegated to oblivion by the insights of the present.

The central act of worship of the people of God is the Eucharist, a service of many names and meanings. It is a fellowship meal, a commemoration of an historical happening, it is an affirmation of the gospel, it is a means by which Christ's disciples are involved in his self-giving in death, crowned and completed in his resurrection. I want to comment on this last aspect of the eucharistic liturgy. The eucharistic offering and the sacrifice of Christ on the cross are rightly linked with the animal sacrifices described in the Old Testament and offered in the temple in the time of Christ. Sacrifice is a language through which men express their worship of God in symbolic action. The offering of animals to God provided a symbolism which enabled the first disciples to enter into the meaning of Christ's death and identify themselves with it. The language of animal sacrifice, however familiar to the ancient world, is obscure and almost meaningless to the twentieth century. But sacrifice has a deep psychological meaning which may help the man of today to enter into this aspect of the Eucharist. For surrender is part of the law of man's spiritual growth. This growth involves the continual letting go, the constant sacrifice of the likes and dislikes of the conscious personality in the interests of the personality as a whole, whose centre is other than the directing ego. There needs to be a continual surrender of values important in the past in order to grasp the values of the centre where God is to be found. The essence of sacrifice is the surrender of the ego-centric will to God who orders our lives from their centre. But weakness and fear hold us back from this surrender. The Eucharist enables us to identify ourselves with Christ's complete sacrifice of his will to the Father. As we receive with faith the eucharistic bread and wine an energy of self-giving is released in us. Only God in me can enable me to let go of my ego-centricity, of my petty anxieties, of my prejudices and antagonisms, and so allow the Spirit to free in me a movement of commitment to God and to my fellows. Through the eucharistic mystery something happens in the people of God which no effort of will could bring about; irrational fears and hates, attractions and repulsions are stirred into consciousness where they can be surrendered and transfigured; the people of God are knit into a more cohesive unity. It is right to simplify the liturgy, to make its meaning more intelligible so that we may share in it with our minds. But what takes place in the Eucharist is ultimately mysterious. And since it is the function of liturgy to make evident what is being enacted, ceremonies that suggest mystery, lights, incense, solemn movement and gesture can play an important part in helping people to enter deeply into the profounder meaning of what is being done.

## THE BODY OF CHRIST

I have taken the people of God as the basic symbol of the Church and drawn out some of its meaning. Corporate prayer takes on a richer significance if it is seen as the assembly of the pilgrim people for mutual encouragement and for the renewal of their commitment. The other two symbols will supplement this foundation image. The first of them is one already mentioned, the Body of Christ. Christ is more than the Leader of the people on trek, like a new Moses or Joshua; his relationship with them is far more intimate than the idea of Leader suggests. St Paul's thought about the relationship of Christ and the people of God veers between two conceptions. Sometimes he thinks of Christ as the Head of the Body and the people of God as the various parts and members of it, sometimes as the whole Body in which all the members are included. It is not necessary to settle for one or other of these conceptions but to let each of them suggest something of the mystery of a relationship which transcends verbal expression. I will briefly draw out the meaning of three ideas contained in it. First, a person is made visible through his body. Through it he expresses his thoughts and feelings, through it he communicates with his fellows, not only by words but often much more powerfully by gesture, by smile or handshake or embrace. Through his body a person influences his fellows and makes an impact on the world around him. The people of God then is the Body through which Christ is present to the world, it is a sign of Christ's presence, a means of his action among men. Is it wholly unrealistic to use language like this in the face of the divisions within the Church and the sins of its members? If we think of the Church as Christ's Body we must admit that it is an ailing body and fails to express more than a faint shadow of the courage and generosity with which Jesus lived his life. But the name by pointing to a future possibility, not yet realized, stimulates the imagination and challenges the will to turn possibility into fact.

The disunity of the people of God is a great obstacle to its acting effectively as Christ's agent in the world. Far more crippling than the organisational disunity and the many denominations is the lack of mutual trust and charity. This is the second idea contained in the image of the Body of Christ. The human body is composed of many parts and organs and of millions of tiny cells, each of which has its own function and cooperates with all the others in movement which is a miracle of harmonious interaction. The lungs breathe in oxygen which is transformed into energy by the body's combustion system. The heart sends blood coursing through all the veins and arteries of the body carrying away used up material and keeping the body clean and healthy. The unity which the healthy body imposes on all its parts and members suggests to St Paul the harmony in which the members of the people of God should work together for the good of all. The members of the body, the hand, the foot, the ear for example, are not equal and interchangeable but complementary. So too the members of the Church have different gifts and different functions. There is no occasion for envy at the supposed superior gifts or position of some, for all have their essential part to play in the healthy working of the Body of Christ. The fact that St Paul has constantly to warn the members of the Church against malice and envy and other faults destructive of unity shows that the Church of his day, like the Church of our own, fell far short of the unity which the body image suggests. Indeed the unity of the Church is not the totalitarian unity imposed willy nilly by the body on its members but a unity that has to be freely chosen. The people of God have to grow up into unity and work to build it. The symbol of the Church as the Body of Christ points to an aim and a task which should impel its members to open themselves to the Spirit who alone can bring the aim and the task to fulfilment.

The third idea to which the body of Christ points is that of the intimate dependence of the Church on Christ. This dependence of Christians on the Lord is a dependence of faith. 'I can do all things through Christ who strengthens me'[3] writes St Paul, who is able to glory in everything that brings home his weakness, because it compels him to rely on Christ who makes him strong. This affirmation by St Paul of the dependence of the Christian on the indwelling Christ is developed further in the teaching of St John's gospel. 'I am the bread of life. He who comes to me shall not hunger and he who believes on me shall never thirst.'[4] The bread of life and the living water are symbols of the knowledge of God in which eternal life consists. The metaphor of eating and drinking enriches the idea of knowing God which Christ mediates. The food and drink that the body takes in and by a process of digestion and metabolism transforms into its own flesh and blood, bone and sinew, suggests a process of spiritual assimilation in which through believing commitment the Christian takes on something of the character of Christ and his own human potential is developed. Through this response to Christ in him he finds himself growing in a relationship of sonship with God.


## THE MOTHER OF BELIEVERS

The symbol of the Church as the body of Christ enriches the basic symbol of the pilgrim people by pointing to the intimate interdependence of the people and its leader and head. The third symbol to fill out the meaning of the pilgrim people is that of Mother, the Mother of believers. The symbol occurs once in the New Testament, in the book of Revelation, in the image of the woman clothed with the sun.[5] But in the early days of the Church the idea of the Church as Mother was familiar. In the *Shepherd of Hermas*, a second century devotional work, which, before the formation of the New Testament canon was looked upon as on a level with the New Testament writings, the Church is depicted as a beautiful and venerable woman. The Church was thought of as the second Eve. Just as the first Eve was the mother of the human race, so the second Eve, sometimes thought of as Mary the Mother of Jesus, sometimes as the Christian Church, is the Mother of all believers. The baptismal font in the ancient liturgy of baptism is seen as a womb from which the new christian was reborn into the family of God's children.

The ideal of the Church as Mother has always been closely associated with that of Mary, the Mother of Jesus; and this conjunction has met a deep human need, the need of a feminine symbol to enable us to grasp the reality of God and his action within us. For God includes within himself both masculine and feminine, and to think of him as purely masculine is seriously to diminish and distort our idea of the Godhead. This one-sidedness cannot be counteracted by any verbal statement, such as that Christ's humanity includes woman as well as man, true though that may be. There is need of a feminine symbol, which by gripping the imagination can stir our depths; and this has been supplied by Mary, the Mother of Jesus. The honour paid to Mary as our Lady, creature like ourselves though she is, is no mere romantic or sentimental devotion but the expression of a deep human need of a concrete figure who can represent to us the motherhood of God. But I believe the figure of Mary is best seen in close association with that of Mother Church of which she is the first and most exalted member. And I believe that there are special reasons today for our returning to this ancient way of understanding the Church.

We have seen that one problem of growth to maturity is that of coming to terms with the tumultuous and traumatic ex-

periences of the first years of life. In the parent dominated
world of early childhood tendencies and attitudes are formed
which commonly persist with only minor modifications into
adult life. Many are handicapped in their relationships with
others because they never knew the experience of being loved
in childhood. In order to love spontaneously we need to have
been loved. The Church is often today spoken of as the loving,
accepting Community in which people can be assured or
reassured that they are accepted and loved and so helped to
grow to their full human stature. One of the reasons for the
small groups of christians who meet together for prayer,
study, discussion or practical action is that this need for warm
acceptance can be better met there than in the relative imper-
sonality of a large congregation. I believe that a return to the
ancient symbol of the Church as the Mother of believers would
add depth and power to the idea of the caring community. It
would call out a response of affection and loyalty not only
towards the great Church spread over the world but for the
local congregation and the small group, for every unit of the
Church should be seen as an embodiment of the whole. It is
true that the idea of Mother Church has been associated with
that of a childishly docile laity, but this is a perversion of the
true conception. For the symbol of the Church as Mother not
only reminds me of my own need of the caring love of the
christian community, it also calls out my own capacity for
caring love as a responsible member of that Community. We
are active members of the mothering Church as well as objects
of the Church's mothering.

This return to the symbol of the Church as Mother is in full
accordance with the contemporary movement to entrust to
women a much fuller share in the Church's ministry than has
been given in the past. This does not necessarily mean ordain-
ing women to the priesthood. For myself I am not convinced
that this would be the best course, despite the strong current
of church opinion in favour of it. If women better than men
symbolise the caring function of the ministry, men better than
women symbolise the directing, guiding function. Men and
women are complementary not interchangeable. The child
needs both father and mother and it is better not to confuse
their functions. For the very large number of Christians who

see the priest as a father who in some sense symbolises God the Father, the idea of women priests must be confusing. For them some other, complementary ministry for women would be better. But the image of the Church as Mother does, I think, tell strongly against the unduly masculine organisation of the Church.

The symbol of the Church as the Mother of believers is congenial to the spirit of the charismatic movement with its stress on the presence and power of the Holy Spirit and its encouragement of free and spontaneous styles of worship. In charismatic worship there seems to occur a release of the childlike spirit. Among the attractive qualities of little children are their spontaneity, the ability to live in the present moment, their capacity for openness and trust, for affection and for rapturous joy. These qualities get suppressed by the demands of school life and the pressure to conform to grown-up standards of behaviour. Bit by bit the spirit of childhood is imprisoned beneath a painfully built up adult attitude. But it lives on underground and is liable to break out when we fall in love or under the influence of that loosener of inhibitions, alcohol. In the free prayer, in the hymns and songs of praise, with their strong rhythm, naively simple words and easily learnt tunes, of charismatic worship people are able to let themselves go and this repressed spirit of childhood sometimes breaks out in delighted praise and spontaneous gratitude and trust. It is likely that much that is childish and uncouth finds expression in this free type of worship. But this is of small significance by comparison with the fact that many find their faith immeasurably deepened and their lives transformed through the atmosphere of faith and fellowship which helps them to let go and to allow their deepest feelings to come out into the open. Through this movement of the Spirit it seems that the pilgrim people is being shown a new way of becoming a true Mother to its members.

In this brief chapter I have hardly touched on the new experiments in corporate worship, the new experimental liturgies or the experiments in the use of mime and dance to express worship. Instead I have attempted the more important task of showing the sacramental character of the Church, the worshipping body; of describing the Church in its many and

various local embodiments as the powerful sign of Christ's
presence in the world. The God who dwells within the centre
of my being dwells equally within my fellows. The various symbols, the people of God, the Body of Christ, the Mother of
believers, by which we grasp the actuality of God's presence
within our fellow worshippers, can bring home the truth not
only that Christ is in us but that we are in him.

1. *Christ the Sacrament* of encounter with God. (Sheed & Ward 1963).
2. *Rebirth of Images* (Dacre Press. 1949) p.20.
3. Colossians 4, 13.2 Corinthians 12.9.
4. John 6, 35.
5. Revelation 12, 1–6.

# 10. Journey's End

This is the use of memory;
For liberation – not less of love but expanding
Of love beyond desire, and so liberation
From the future as well as the past.
                                    T.S. Eliot, *Little Gidding* ll. 156–159

Following an old tradition I have spoken of human life as a journey. The journey begins in the mists of infancy, passes through the changing scenery of childhood, across the forests, moors and swamps of adolescence, through the settled and civilised regions of adulthood, to the descent through quiet valleys or down wind-swept hills to the shore of the great sea where our journey ends. But if life can be likened to a journey it must also be seen as a growing thing like a tree. The seed of the tree is sown in the soil, it puts down root into the earth and pushes up a green shoot into the light; it grows first into a slender sapling and then into the flexible strength of a great tree, rooted in the earth and stretching out branches towards the sky. The image of the tree complements that of the journey. The seed of life is sown through the coming together of man and woman and the exchange which effects the union of male and female sperm to become the nucleus of the embryo in the womb. After being carried for nine months in his mother's body the infant is born, helpless and totally dependent, but, fostered by the love and care of parents, grows apace. So far growth has been automatic and the infant has no choice but to grow. He is carried along wherever the stream of life bears him. But gradually he learns to will and choose so that though his growth continues willy nilly he is able in minute degree to modify the direction and perhaps the pace of growth. As we grow older our own choices and decisions play an increasing part in the manner of our growth and the kind of person we grow into. Then the image of a journey which we choose to undertake becomes an increasingly appropriate picture of life. It is not, of course, open to us to refuse the journey. What becomes increasingly within our power is the ability to choose where we will go. Whichever way we choose we travel always towards the unknown, though this is much more obvious in some lives than in others. For we can never see even at our most clear-sighted more than a short distance ahead. However we calculate the probabilities, the unexpected and the unforeseeable occur which throw all our forecasts out. It may be possible for a man to plot fairly accurately the course of his career. But can he equally accurately foresee how his domestic life, or his friendships, or his out of work interests, or his health, or his spiritual concern will flourish or fail? In one or other or all of these areas he is likely to be taken by surprise by the unexpected and the unforeseen.

## GROWTH TOWARDS WHOLENESS

My belief expressed in this book is that the whole of man's life is lived whether consciously or unconsciously in the presence of God. This is true of all, believers and atheists, religious and irreligious alike. Noone, I believe, is without the unseen, fostering, influence of God pressing him towards his self-realization in whatever way however unlikely, this can best be achieved. But I believe that it is an advantage beyond price for a person to be able to realize this Presence and consciously respond to it, to be able to rely on a Wisdom and Strength greater than his own and to try to follow the direction in which divine Wisdom guides and divine Strength enables. Earlier I spoke of the probability that many who do not profess belief in God do nevertheless rely on him and follow his guidance under some other name, or perhaps without any name at all. It would also seem that there are those who do profess to believe in God but do not consciously either seek his guidance or rely on his grace. All the same, despite the loose ends and general untidiness, the imponderables and the unexplainables, that characterise human life it is an immense blessing for a person to realise his life as resting in the hand of God, of One who with unsleeping care is pressing him to grow to his full human stature, to grow into one who can relate to him as a son to a Father. This is journey's end as I see it: to have reached, by whatever strange vicissitudes a lasting relationship to the Creator of all that is. We could never hope to reach this end if God had not set himself to lead us there. We could not find our way without immense help from God all through life, given through innumerable agencies, events and circumstances. Nor can we reach life's goal unless we want it and freely choose it.

I have described the goal of life as a deep and lasting relationship to God. But this relationship cannot be under-stood apart from two other relationships which are bound up with it, with other people and with ourselves. Indeed the relationship to God, to other people and to ourselves forms a trinity in unity. Each relationship requires and depends upon the others, so that if one is defective the others will be defective too. It is through other people's love that God's love is first mediated to us. To attempt to be open to God and closed to our fellows is to drive uphill with all our brakes on. But equally important is it for me to come to terms with the whole of myself. My own personality to begin with is an unplumbed mystery as much to myself as to others. It may indeed be so totally unknown that I may not have an inkling that there is anything to know. I should then be like a man who all un-knowingly carries about in his hand luggage a poisonous snake or a bomb that explodes on impact. We come bit by bit through the processes of growing up and establishing our selves in our social world to know ourselves better. The task of exploring the unknown continent of our total personality is best done in middle life or later. Introspection can be a danger for those who are not fairly firmly established in social relationships. Like the youth Narcissus in the greek myth who fell in love with his own beauty a person may become so interested in his own depths that he has no energy available for forming friendships or for the other tasks of life. Further we grow in self-awareness not only by introspection but by tackling the jobs that lie to hand, by measuring our strength and skill against taxing work and difficult people. In middle and later life after the heat of the struggle to succeed is over and such measure of success as we have attained has lost all its novelty and most of its charm, then especially we are ready to devote energy to the task of gaining deeper self-awareness. Until we know ourselves we cannot really possess ourselves. And until we possess ourselves and have the inner peace that comes from self-possession we shall find it impossible to relate to other people except either by trying to possess and dominate them or by letting them possess or dominate us.

## MOVEMENT OF METANOIA

The human journey rightly understood is a movement of *metanoia*. Repentance, the usual translation of this Greek word, is an unsatisfactory one, because it too much suggests self-blame and the acknowledgment of sin, instead of hope which is its essential characteristic. The word means literally change of mind or change of attitude; and though self-blame and the realization of guilt may prepare the way for *metanoia* it is hope that brings about the change of heart and mind which effects a new orientation in a person's life. In the story of the prodigal son it was hope that set the young man on the journey home, though it was his state of spiritual destitution and wretchedness that brought him to the point of *metanoia*. If we are right in seeing with John Hick the perfection of man not as something from which we have fallen in primeval times but as something to be striven for, a goal to be achieved in the future, then hope rather than self-blame or sorrow for sin is all the more plainly the primary incentive in the human journey. The hope that will enable effective *metanoia* includes the hope of becoming more and more completely what in essence we are, of living our own truth to the full; but it includes also the hope of cooperating with our fellows in building a society favourable to growth in humanity; it will include the hope of a city where men will live at peace with men, where the natural environment will be cared for and not recklessly exploited, where men will have learnt to live together as a family because they worship a common Father and Creator.

To insist on hope as the mainspring of *metanoia* does not as we have seen ignore the fact of human evil, of man's perversity and blindness, his arrogance, cruelty and sloth and his timid refusal to respond to the summons to change. But psychology makes for a merciful view of human sin, and without condoning wrong-doing makes it possible to feel compassion for the sinner and to hope that divine mercy will heal and forgive him as we pray that our sin may be forgiven and healed.

Two other aspects of the journey, both of them touched on earlier in the book, help to fill in the picture. We have seen it as a movement towards union with the transcendent God. But God our Creator guides us and acts upon us from within our own being. We draw near to him as we submit to the sway of an inner magnet, the heart's heart, the deep centre. The Godward journey is a movement of centring, of integration, which happens partly of itself, partly through our conscious consent. At the outset of the journey and for a long time the pull of the centre is not perceived for what it is. But its force is as powerful as is the gravitational pull of the moon on the earth's oceans, causing the ebb and flow of the tides. One effect of the influence of the Centre is the pendulum swing of opposing moods and impulses, the alternation of elation and despair, of going out to others and withdrawing into one's shell. It is the gravitational pull of the centre, acting as a balancing factor within the total personality, that causes this oscillation of opposites. The centring process takes place partly through a surrender of represssions, through the letting go of bottled up rage or fear or hate or despair. First I become conscious of these violent feelings and acknowledge them as my own and then I let them go without either acting them out or trying to get rid of them; I just endure them until gradually they wither. As I do this I experience a strange enlargement of consciousness, I feel larger, humbler, less self-confident and more open to the centre. I become at the same time more myself than ever before and also, paradoxically, more at the disposal of other people and more the servant of the centre.

As a counterpart to the centring process which draws a person to become increasingly at home with the forces and energies of his own being, there tends to develop a new attitude to the world outside him, the world of people and events, of nature and the arts. He finds himself growing both in appreciation of and detachment from the external world. Less and less does he look outside himself either for reassurance or to impress others; and with this decline of self-preoccupation there grows a deeper and more sympathetic appreciation of people and of the whole realm of facts, ideas and values. This is part of *metanoia*, of a change of attitude, of a reaching out in hope to God, whether or not it is consciously realized to be such. It is a movement of worship, of acknowledging and honouring God, by responding to the signs by which he discloses himself to us. The response will set free our innate longing to be one with God from the idolatries, the undue valuation of and possessive attachment to persons and objects, which divert it from its true goal. The purification and rectification of our deepest aspirations will lead to a growing concern for what is real, true and genuine and an increasing distaste for the unreal, the shoddy and the sham. It will bring about a growing appreciation of and love for the humanity and the special qualities and strengths of others, and a firmer desire and determination to act justly and generously, to face trouble courageously, to meet human need with compassion, energy and gentleness. This liberation from undue self-concern which enables a person to see the world around him with new eyes is likely also to awaken in him a keener perception of and delight in beauty. No doubt the manner and extent of the flowering of a man's aesthetic sensibility will depend much on its previous education. In this sphere as in many others the rule 'to him that hath shall be given' applies. But I believe joy in beauty is intensified for those who are able to recognise beautiful sights and sounds as heralds of God, the uncreated Beauty.

I have described human life both as a journey in hope towards a great and blessed goal beyond our horizon, and as a threefold growth in relationship with other people, with our own depths and with God. But it is possible for me to evade my true destination or get lost on the way, and it is possible for my growth in relationship to be stunted or distorted. What can I do to rectify my distorted relationships, whether these are the consequence of unfortunate circumstances or of my own folly or perversity? What can I do to get back on to the road leading to my true destiny if I have strayed from it and got lost? The road towards our true destiny is the way of hope in God, but it cannot be trodden by those burdened too heavily by the past. Luggage from the past must be reduced to manageable proportions if we are to carry it where our true destiny beckons. The weight of the past consists of memories, of tendencies, habits and attitudes which we acquired in trying to adjust ourselves to events of long ago. This need not necessarily be a burden or a handicap. It is the past actions and happenings which we cling to in fear, despair or self-complacence, perhaps without knowing it, that prevent our going forward. I touched on this need to let go of the past in a previous chapter (chap. 7) where I likened it to a kind of dying. I want to go more thoroughly into this now.


## LOOKING BACK

One of the tasks of later life, more especially for the years of retirement, is to look back at the joys and sorrows, the successes and failures, the unresolved problems and the un-finished tasks of the past; to look back in order to let go. Only by so doing is it possible to loosen the clutch of the past and travel forward in hope. It is easiest to begin with the obvious blessings and undoubted successes, but it is even more im-portant to face the disasters, the anguish, the failures, the sin that lie behind us: to face both bane and blessing and to let both go. For a man who has some genuine faith in God the best way to face the past is by thanksgiving to God. If I thank God, for example, for the love and care of my father and mother when I was small, not only do I bring an old and perhaps forgotten warmth into my relationship with God, but my childish dependence on parents who cannot now help me is transformed into a reliance on God who can; I am letting go of the dead past and attaching myself to God in the living present. It is equally important to let go of the perhaps quite minor successes that fed my vanity or the position which helped me to feel important or the rare moments of ecstatic joy or triumph. Nostalgia for an imagined paradise in the past can prevent me from grasping real happiness in the present. Gratitude to God is a sovereign remedy for clinging to the past for those who can express it with sincerity. But what of the resentments and sense of guilt that haunt us out of our past? Humiliation and self-blame, wrongs committed by us and wrongs inflicted on us, can chain us more firmly to the past and prevent us advancing in hope more effectively even than the wistful dwelling on past happiness and success. It is more painful to recall these hours of agony and distress than the times of enjoyment, but recalled they need to be if we are to be free of them. T.S. Eliot has written of:

'the rending pain of re-enactment
Of all that you have done, and been; the shame
Of motives late revealed, and the awareness
Of things ill done and done to others' harm
Which once you took for exercise of virtue.
Then fools' approval stings, and honour stains.'[1]

Is it possible to look back on our misdeeds with gratitude to God? We may not perhaps be able to thank God for our failures, our betrayals, our wasted opportunities or the injustice of which we were the victim. But if I believe that God is everywhere at work bringing good out of evil, building success out of disaster, refining character through suffering, teaching wisdom through failure, then I can thank God for what he was doing and is continuing to do to redeem the past.

I would like to suggest one possible method of facing the past in order to prevent its paralysing us in the present. In three chapters of this book I have described some of the tasks of life, beginning with those of childhood and going on through adolescence to the responsibilities of adulthood. In confronting our own past I would suggest reversing the procedure. Beginning from where we are we would then look back at the most recent phase of our lives, recalling the good and the bad and the mixed, soaking ourselves in it and then letting it all go in thanksgiving. Having done our best to remember and surrender the doings and happenings of our latest period, I would suggest going phase by phase, period by period right back to childhood. The divisions of the phases will inevitably be somewhat arbitrary and artificial, for life is continuous. But in most lives, I think, there is a sufficient number of convenient milestones to make it possible to divide our life into stretches of a length suitable for the exercise we are describing. Change of work, retirement, change of residence, bereavement, the growing up of a family, may mark the divisions of the later years of life. The earlier years are marked by the successive stages of education, of going to work, of getting established in a job or career, of getting married. Looking back I recall the houses I have lived in, the people I have known, my close relatives and intimate friends, those who were antipathetic or antagonistic to me, my work and my leisure occupations, my illnesses and accidents, my pain and pleasure, my success and failure, my recurrent moods, my shortcomings, my sins. I believe it is best to dwell at some length on each phase before turning to an earlier one. For a thorough recall of the more recent period prepares for the more difficult and perhaps more important recollecting of what lies further back.

The exercise I have described in outline is only one possible method of coming to terms with the past. Many will dislike so systematic a procedure and will prefer to move about from moment to moment in the past, from personality to personality, from one period to another as they may be prompted by intuition or some felt need, without regard to chronology. Others will feel the need to talk over the happenings of the past with some understanding person. The idea of settling accounts with the past is not new. The proverbial saying, 'Count your blessings', points to one aspect of the settlement. There is also the practice of making a general confession of all the sins of one's past life. But neither of these practices fully meets the need to face the past honestly and squarely. For life's ills have to be faced as well as its blessings, and we are troubled not only by our sins but by misfortune and wrongs inflicted on us.

## LOOKING FORWARD

Letting go of the past is a way of describing a movement by
which past experience becomes more closely integrated with
the present, by which blockages from the past which are interfering with the free flow of the current of life are removed. It
is part of the individuation process described earlier.
Thanksgiving for the past automatically fosters an attitude of
hope towards the future. For the more conscious we are of
God's guiding hand in the past the more we shall come to
count on it for the future. 'Old men ought to be explorers'
writes T.S. Eliot. Too often, he observes, they are timid and
querulous.

> 'Do not let me hear
> Of the wisdom of old men, but rather of their folly,
> Their fear of fear and  frenzy, their fear of possession,
> Of belonging to another, or to others, or to God.' [2]

The poet's words were aimed at those of his contemporaries
who, not having found a meaning in life, were disturbed at the
prospect of death. But not all the old are afraid of death, many
face its approach with tranquillity and some look forward to it
with hope. Nor is the fear of death only an affliction of the
old. The young are sometimes haunted by the idea of impending death. On one occasion I remember a university
student telling me that he had this fear and that sometimes he
would wake at night in a panic that he was about to die. I
mentioned this to a psychiatrist friend who replied 'Fear of
death means fear of life.' The next time I saw the student I
repeated what the psyciatrist had said: 'Fear of death means
fear of life.' The words struck him like a blow in the face; their
aptness left him for the moment speechless. Fear of death may
be a fear of the unknown demands of life which threaten to
destroy old securities and remove old supports. But if anxiety
about death in the young is often a shrinking from impending
change, among the old death looms up as a visitor who may
come any day and is certain to come before long.
   Facing death as a friend is easier for those who believe in a
life beyond death. Jung has written 'As a physician I am con-

vinced that it is hygienic – if I may use the word – to discover in death a goal towards which one can strive; and that shrinking away from it is something unhealthy and abnormal which robs the second half of life of its purpose.' 'From the standpoint of psychotherapy it would therefore be desirable to think of death as only a transition – one part of a life-process whose extent and duration escape our knowledge.'[3] It is desirable to think of death in this way, but what is desirable is not always true. The question of life after death is nagging the minds of many today. The interest in the investigations of the Society for  Psychical Research as also the attempts to make contact with the dead through psychic sensitives bears witness to a widespread concern about what lies beyond death.

The christian belief in a life to come is part of his faith in God. The life to come as he understands it is to be thought of rather as the resurrection of the whole person than as merely the survival of bodily death, though it must include this. Let us call on Austin Farrer for the last time to express the christian view point with his accustomed clarity. 'Belief in resurrection is belief not in ourselves but in God who raises us. It is in fact the acid test of whether we believe in God or not. A God who raises the dead is a real power; he is not just a fanciful name for the order of nature, whether physical or moral. A God so identified with the natural order that he adds nothing to it is difficult to distinguish from the world he rules or the laws that govern it'[4] Again Farrer writes: 'We ask what God means by bringing up a creature capable of immortal hope; capable besides of drawing on the source of everlasting renewal by a personal and voluntary attachment to his Creator. Does not the Maker show his hand? Is there not an implicit promise of, immortalization in the nature of such a creature as this?'[5] This last argument weighs heavily with me. The whole drive of human life, as illuminated by the christian revelation, is towards a greater and more intimate attachment to the transcendent God who addresses us from many directions and through countless media. Through this growing attachment we become more and more truly at one in ourselves and at one with our fellows and increasingly devoted to the true, the good, the beautiful. I do not believe that our Author having brought us thus far will be content to let us slip back into nothingness.

In death we face the unknown and I believe we can confront it with hope as well as courage. In his *Utopia* Sir Thomas More describes an imaginary race of islanders who lived without benefit of the christian revelation a life lit only by reason. The attitude of the Utopians to death is strikingly different from that of most people today. 'They do mourn and lament every man's sickness but no man's death, unless it be one whom they see depart from his life carefully and against his will. For this they take for a very evil token, as though the soul being in despair and vexed in conscience, through some privy and secret forefeeling of the punishment now at hand were afraid to depart. They therefore who see this kind of death do abhor it and they who so die they bury with sorrow and silence. Contrariwise all that depart merrily and full of good hope, for these no man mourneth, but followeth the hearse with joyful singing, commending the soul to God with great affection.'[6] The Utopians understood how to rejoice in the present but to let it go and face the future with hope. They suggest how those who believe in God should face the end of their earthly journey in dignity and hope, hope not in man's innate survival power but in the Creator who called him into a relationship with himself. In the opening paragraph of this chapter I likened our life to a journey which ends on the shore of the sea. The sea is a symbol of death, but it is also a symbol of God himself. Death is too great an unknown for us to be able to face it without a tremor; but the believer can face journey's end in hope because he can rely on the God whose presence all through life's journey he has learnt to recognize. Let us leave the last word to T.S. Eliot:

'We must be still and still moving
Into another intensity
For a further union, a deeper communion
Through the dark cold and the empty desolation,
The wave cry, the wind cry, the vast waters
Of the petrel and the porpoise. In my end is my beginning.'[7]

1. *Little Gidding*, II. 138–143.
2. *East Coker*, II. 113–116.

3. *Modern Man in Search of a Soul.* (Kegan Paul, Trench, Trubner & Co. 1936) p. 129.
4. *Saving Belief.* p. 141.
5. Op. cit. p. 148
6. Book 2. Of the Religions in Utopia.
7. *East Coker.* ll. 204–209.